LIFE, LOVE AND LEGACY

CASSANDRA FARMER

Unless indicated all scripture references are from the King James Version, New International Version, and English Standard versions of the Bible, used by permission. Scripture quotations are from the ESV Bible copyright 2001

ISBN:

Printed in the USA

Forward

There are few people who could suffer a loss such as Cassandra has and remain as loving and giving as she is. In this first work she discusses the hurt and pain she experienced but also the love and joy she found in the love of her family and her God. This story of struggle and success, love and loss and legacy will make you cry, laugh and lift your head, knowing that you can make it through anything!

Cassandra's passion for life is evident in every word. Her tenacity will inspire you to continue to work, to pray and to live your life more abundantly. Thank you Cassandra for your transparency. It was my absolute pleasure to help you bring your story to a world that needs to hear it

Almena Mayes

Owner and CEO

Cre8 Your Reality Publishing

In the Beginning...

I remember what the backyard on Knot Street where we lived briefly in Shelby, NC looked like when dark; lots of kudzu, empty, and only one street light. There was lots of yelling, someone breaking a television, and for a while I thought it was just a dream—the color pink, a simple chiffon dress that gathered at the bust.

Although I was very young, some things, like her voice, stuck with me forever. I remember her singing while cooking. This memory replays itself in my mind, in my spirit and in my heart. My third birthday was only five weeks away when my entire world changed. Through my innocent my little world was filled the calm moments of my mom cooking and singing in the kitchen. But, there are also memories of things like the television being thrown and busted, someone being chased and running for her life, horrible fights and crying.

That was my norm. Then, both parents were gone in a matter of moments. One was dead and the other was headed to prison. I didn't understand what was happening but I knew I was being left behind. I WAS LOST, FORGOTTEN, DEPRESSED, SCARED, NERVOUS, UNSURE, ANXIOUS, LESS THAN, ALONE, DAMAGED GOODS, HURT, ORPHANED, AND NOT GOOD ENOUGH.

I not only survived this but I have thrived. How did I make it? I took solace in the things that soothed my soul, the scriptures and quotes that inspired me. It is my honor to share them with you. Prayerfully, you have not experienced the pain that I have, and these words will simply give you an extra boost. However, if you have suffered as I have suffered, may they give you the strength to carry on, the hope for a better tomorrow and the faith to believe that it will all change for the better.

Wards of the Court...

Matthew 6:26 ESV

Look at the birds of the air: they neither sow nor reap nor gather into barns, and yet your heavenly Father feeds them. Are you not of more value than they?

Merriam-Webster defines value as relative worth, utility, or importance. At two years and 11 months old, on a Sunday evening, March 10, 1974, I felt my life and my one-year-old brother's life must not have been too important to God.
In a matter of moments, we became wards of the court.

On a beautiful, lazy Sunday evening after Sunday dinner and a few television shows, my grandmother and grandfather were relaxing in the back room. Grandma was on the phone talking to her oldest daughter, who was married and lived up north. My mother had just put my brother down to sleep, but I was still up stirring around in the front with her. I'm not sure what my mother and her sister Cookie were doing, but I was always told they were the best of friends.

My estranged father, Freddie, told me years later that he was there at our home to visit my mother. He was estranged because he was very abusive, jealous man. It didn't matter who was around or what happened. If any man, and I do mean ANY man no matter age or race, looked in my mother's direction or said anything to her, my father immediately blamed her for the attention.

He wasn't a good provider. Often, we lacked the necessities. Things like milk, diapers and food were always scarce. My mother was only 19 years old. She tried to work but had to leave her job and get her family to what she felt was safety. She returned home with her two children.

That evening, my Father hid in our backyard and waited until my Uncle left for work. Then, he entered the house and started a fight with my mother. She grabbed a butcher knife to protect herself while my Aunt Cookie, to help her sister, jumped in between them. My father took the knife from my mother, reached over her baby sister and stabbed her in the jugular vein. My mother bled to death in her baby sister's arms. I was still in the room. There is no way I could understand what had happened. It all happened so quickly. By the time my grandparents and my Aunt Linda heard what was going on, my mother was gone. My Father sat there, crying over what he had done. He didn't try to escape. He waited for the cops to pick him up.

In those few but very traumatic and horrific moments, my brother and I became wards of the court. We had no idea what had truly happened other than our beautiful mother, who was always there, was gone. I turned three the next month.

I cried a lot growing up. I am told that my brother, at times, did the same. We had no idea how traumatized we were. We needed more help than anyone in our family could honestly give us.

Nearly half the women murdered worldwide are murdered by a spouse or significant other. Not much is known about what happens to the children after such a horrible event. I guess people just don't want to talk about it. It's way too painful. The trauma of homicide can lead to several other issues. I struggled with the memories, anxiety, problems sleeping and self-destructive behaviors. I'm sure my brother did as well, but that's his story to tell.

My grandparents had already lost their oldest son to the Vietnam War, so losing another child was definitely more than they could take. They had already reared their own children and were finally feeling a bit of relief financially. How in the world could they rear two BABIES? Whatever their norm was up until this point was no more. Between them they only had a 6th grade education. However, my grandmother later earned her GED. How were they going to handle all of our expenses AND mental trauma? But God!

My grandmother said that she was introduced to God early in life. Although her family lacked money and other resources, God still provided all that they truly needed. They had their faith in God above all other things. As she got old enough to have her own family of five children, she held onto her faith in God. She went through several medical crises and was even told she wouldn't walk again due to rheumatoid arthritis. But, she did learn to walk again. God carried her through a lot, and even though she told me years later, she begged for God to take her after my mother was killed, she took on the task of raising us! She asked God how He could have taken another child from her. She said she asked Him to show her what He needed of her. She knew there was message or mission she needed to complete because through it, He still provided, and she was still alive.

Our maternal family fought to gain custody of my brother and me. Through no fault of our own, it was left up to the court to decide where we would call home. Other family members and friends offered the help they could. The thought was that one baby would be enough to handle in any household. They almost split us up. My grandmother said, no! She said that we were all that God had left her of her daughter, and she wanted to keep us together. She had no clue where the funding or other resources would come from, but God had never failed her. Her faith was enough because God's track record was excellent.

Growing up with that type of love and faith, there was no way it wouldn't reach us. On the phone with my brother Freddie, Jr. we shared the good news that God has given us! This year, 2020, has brought about many challenges for several families. People have lost several of their friends and loved ones. Some have lost their jobs, and others have not seen their loved ones since March or more due to the rules, regulations, and risks of Covid-19. Amid this pandemic, there are still blessings and miracles happening every day! Many have suffered the dreaded diagnosis but still survived. Conversely, have remained healthy (currently, my immediate family and my brother's immediate family). Some have kept their jobs, traveled, and have received financial successes and miracles. We are still blessed. Because of the experiences my grandparents have shared, and I saw them go through, it has caused my faith to remain strong! I'm human; yes, there are times I've cried or become anxious when life throws me a curveball. But, when I pray and settle myself, have a conversation with God, and meditate to give him room to speak to my soul, it calms me. I remember who He is. He is________? You fill in the blank with whatever you need Him to be. Why? Because He is everything, you'll ever need! He is the only one who can heal you, keep you, get you through whatever your situation may be and strengthen you. HE IS THE ONE!

Thought of the Day

"How many of us still live by the phrase 'If only'...when God has said, 'I already'?

Brian Logue

When was there a time in your life when you felt left alone and could not see your way through a difficult situation?

Looking back on this situation, where can you see that God was with you?

What's on the Inside

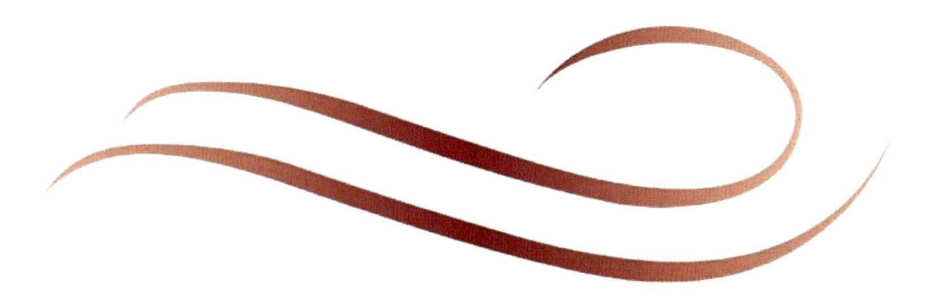

<u>1 Corinthians 6:19-20</u> ESV

Or do you not know that your body is a temple of the Holy Spirit within you, whom you have from God? You are not your own, for you were bought with a price. So glorify God in your body.

This scripture hit home with me when I finally realized the many messes I had gotten myself into looking for love. Having a father who wasn't present to have the father/ daughter talk about men and their way of thinking or experiencing being a daddy's girl who was treasured and protected caused me to make some impulsive decisions.

To truly understand this scripture, you must understand the love God has for us and ALL that He did to SHOW us His love. "You are not your own; you were bought with a price." That struck me! I became aware that the shell, the bodies we live in, aren't to be used for our pleasures, to glorify ourselves or be defiled. Our bodies are to be used for God's glory. It doesn't matter what stage of life we're in, married, or single. Whenever making decisions involving our bodies, we must stop and think, "is this something that will bring God glory?"

I can't tell you how often I paid more attention to what a person TOLD me rather than what that person SHOWED me. I know seems suspicious and unbelievable that someone would show you the most courageous form of love-- die for you. It's especially so when you've done absolutely NOTHING to deserve it. Who does that? After all the mistakes I've made, the selfish decisions that hurt not only myself but those I cared for deeply, Jesus still sacrificed Himself for me! Here's the kicker. He knew about every one of my transgressions. He knows about all of us! He created us and knew at our conception what we would do. God knows all our dirty little secrets and lies. Still, he sent His son to die for us.

After being incarcerated for fifteen years, my father was released around my eighteenth birthday. I was a toddler when he went to jail but a young woman when he came home. Because he was not in my life as I grew up and began dating, in his absence, I looked to the men I dated for the unconditional love I saw other girls receive from their dads. I knew these guys weren't my father, but I needed what I thought they could provide. I didn't know how it felt to be a daddy's girl— to have a man to love and protect you at all costs. I had never experienced love from one who wanted nothing from me but would do anything to ensure I was loved the way I should be. Yes, I had my grandfather and uncle in my life, and they loved me in the ways they could. But as one of the children left behind after our mother's horrific death and my father's immediate incarceration, there was a huge hole that couldn't be filled by anyone else. My family loved us tremendously. The sacrifices made for my brother and me would have never been made if they had not. Unfortunately, the love of a parent can never be replaced by anyone else; no matter how hard anyone tries.

It is important that we take care of the beautiful souls God has blessed us with. Since my late forties, and for the last several years of my life, I've felt like my body has betrayed me. If you're anything like me, nothing looks the same. This is the reason why I didn't say beautiful bodies. Instead I said, beautiful souls. Somehow, after my thirties, I believe I fell asleep, and someone switched bodies with me because everything appears to be going south really quickly! How our bodies look is mostly due to genetics and what we choose to put in them. When I look at my birthday suit, I see one that looks exactly like my grandmother's. Don't get me wrong, as a BBW, I still can make a pair of jeans walk and a dress sway so beautifully you'd think it was a summer breeze blowing on a cold December morning! But, according to how I feel throughout the day, I know I'm not at my best. I tire easily, and my energy levels aren't quite as high as they should be. Is this good for the Kingdom? How am I bringing glory to God when my weight issues are wearing me out? How am I fulfilling my purpose when I can't even accomplish the mission God has for me? I love to travel. To do so comfortably means I need to drop several pounds. I have no desire to be the passenger who oozes into the seat next to me or needs an extension for her seatbelt! I've got work to do! We all do! Mentally and physically, all of who we are, including the shell we dwell in, belongs to God and is meant for His mission and glory!

Thought of the Day

It is health that is real wealth and not pieces of Gold and Silver. ~Mahatma Gandhi

In what ways do you honor God in your relationships?

What do you feed your mind spiritually daily to ensure you're mentally healthy?

What are you doing daily to ensure you're physically healthy?

The Woman Who Fears the Lord...

Proverbs 31: 10-31

10

An excellent wife who can find?

She is far more precious than jewels.

11

The heart of her husband trusts in her,

and he will have no lack of gain.

12

She does him good, and not harm,

all the days of her life.

13

She seeks wool and flax,

and works with willing hands.

14

She is like the ships of the merchant;

she brings her food from afar.

15

She rises while it is yet night

and provides food for her household

and portions for her maidens.

16

She considers a field and buys it;

with the fruit of her hands, she plants

a vineyard.

17

She dresses herself[b] with strength

and makes her arms strong.

18

She perceives that her merchandise is

profitable.

Her lamp does not go out at night.

19

She puts her hands to the distaff,

and her hands hold the spindle.

20

She opens her hand to the poor

and reaches out her hands to the needy.

21

She is not afraid of snow for her household,

for all her household are clothed in scarlet.[c]

22

She makes bed coverings for herself;

her clothing is fine linen and purple.

23

Her husband is known in the gates

when he sits among the elders of the land.

24

She makes linen garments and sells them;

she delivers sashes to the merchant.

25

Strength and dignity are her clothing,

and she laughs at the time to come.

26

She opens her mouth with wisdom,

and the teaching of kindness is on her tongue.

27

She looks well to the ways of her household

and does not eat the bread of idleness.

28

Her children rise up and call her blessed;

her husband also, and he praises her:

29

"Many women have done excellently,

but you surpass them all."

30

Charm is deceitful, and beauty is vain,

but a woman who fears the Lord is to be praised.

31

Give her of the fruit of her hands,

and let her works praise her in the gates.

This is my grandmother, Louise Lockhart Gill! What a Queen! I tell people that if I can become half the woman she was, I will have succeeded. She wasn't just a grandmother to me; she spent thirty years rearing my baby brother and me. Instead of empty nesting and letting us become wards of the court, she dedicated her life to loving us and teaching us the essential things that can't be bought. She demonstrated what happens when God is the center of all that you do.

I lovingly called her Momma. Momma had my Daddy (grandfather Edward) spoiled! There was no other woman he completely shared his deepest concerns or joy with. He wouldn't even eat another person's cooking. As we used to say, Momma could burn! She was an excellent cook!

During all my years of waking up in the morning and going to school, Momma had breakfast ready and dinner waiting. There were very few days in the week that we ate cereal or oatmeal (old fashion, not instant). Oatmeal was our favorite "fast food" for breakfast. Most days, we woke up to homemade biscuit bread we called "who' cake" for "whole cake." LOL!!! When we said it, it sounded like "hoe cake." Jesus, help us! We were running around happy with our lips smacking, telling our friends about the homemade bread momma makes for us. Of course, those who had their birth parents looked at us like we were crazy!

She would have homemade cornbread too for dinner, depending on what she had on the menu. Her cornbread melted in your mouth. It was sweet enough not to taste like cake. It was buttery and smooth with a crunch on the outside. To this day, I love the smell of homemade bread! I could go on and on about the pastries, cakes, and other sides with tasty meats she cooked. For me, all of it is, the smell of love. As a mother myself, I realize the work she put into feeding us all. Still, she worked a full-time job, was a missionary at church, and was our number one cheerleader in everything we did as children.

Momma was great at pumping you up to do something we were scared to do. She knew these were positive moves and ones we would grow from. I call her the Ultimate Agent. She was an encouraging woman but would also put us on the spot and volunteer us to do things in church or school. I hated that because I was timid. She did everything possible to help me do things I was afraid of. It showed me I was stronger than I gave myself credit for.

Early Saturday mornings were spent going to the farmers' market. With the windows down and the cool morning air blowing across our faces, my brother and I would ride in the back seat as Momma and Daddy drove us to the market before the sun came up. They would arrive greeting their friends who farmed locally. They only purchased the perishables because Daddy grew everything else. We had relatives that had cows, chickens, pigs, etc. I'm not trying to offend the non-meat eaters, but that's how we survived.

After going to the farmer's market, we'd go shopping downtown at Sears & Roebuck, A V Wray's, and Hudson's. One of Momma's favorite things to do was finding the perfect lace on a new slip and the finest hosiery to match her Sunday attire. Oh yes, she was a slip wearing, hosiery and glove, largest designer hat-wearing sistah! She never left the house without looking her best, lipstick included. Yes, even to the grocery store. I loved that about her!

When time allowed, Momma went back to school to get her GED. She reared my brother and me on a 6th-grade education. I watched her negotiate business, speak on her family's behalf when needed, and stay on her knees talking to God about EVERYTHING! In sadness and happiness, she praised God. As the last young lady she reared, I didn't realize until she was nearing death that Momma had been preparing me for womanhood all my life. I was taught and raised to leave the room full of men to sit and learn from the women in the room. I was told that no matter what I saw or heard, I was to sit quietly because, as a child, I needed to stay in a child's place. I was not allowed to interrupt adults; if so, I was slapped in the mouth for doing so (especially when she took the time to warn me). Even now, I remember sitting on our front porch that faced the ball field we played on all during summer. Momma and her close friend Bonita (the spelling may be wrong) would be talking about their highs and lows of the day, their concerns in life, and encouraging each other. Where did that go? Not many of us ladies do that today.

It was dusk and the summer breeze carried all the scents of the flowers that were in bloom around the house that Momma told Daddy to plant. LOL! They'd fuss about what to plant and when, but Daddy always followed what Momma told him. He'd do all the work tending to them and his beautiful large garden. Then, he'd say Momma took all the credit for each bloom or produce. It was their way; their song and dance. She studied her husband well and knew exactly how to reach him when no one else could.

My final walk with Momma began in 1998 and ended in 2001. She was diagnosed with lung cancer. Momma was a mill worker at Esther Mill for many years. The day the doctor shared the news with her, Daddy, Uncle Smokie (Sherwood) and I were there. I'll never forget it. It was a gorgeous, sunlit day. The hospital boasted a beautifully manicured lawn and was full of beautiful flowers. After the doctor gave her the diagnosis, we sat silently in the room in disbelief. Momma broke the silence with the one question we all wanted to ask but couldn't. She asked, "So doc, how long do I have? I know you can only tell me what you've studied. but my belief in what God can do outweighs what you're about to tell me. Still, how long?" At that time, most people were told that you have about 3-6 months to live. She was told the same. The doctor gave her all her options and, of course, left her with the decision of how to proceed. We left the office, walked through the lobby of the hospital, and out to the lawn.

While standing in this beautiful blue sunny sky, we were all so shaken…everyone but Momma! She immediately said to us all, well, I'm thinking about treatment to hopefully give us more time. BUT!!! I'M GOING TO LIVE UNTIL I DIE!!! And we went on with the rest of the day living life as she said she would. She prayed, and she got sick at times. She prayed and kept working until she couldn't. She prayed and kept teaching me how to cook several of her specialties and even made me promise that when she left here, I would make sure we had Thanksgiving and Christmas dinners for Daddy until he passed. There were times people would try to come and visit her, and she would even be home. Momma still visited others that were sick and cared for those who couldn't care for themselves. She had become a private nurse—her last assignment.

Momma lived for another three years and six months after her diagnosis. She outlived the doctor that diagnosed her and another doctor's father, who also passed with cancer. Momma went on a cruise each year after begging her doctor to release her for just enough time to enjoy herself because we had a nurse in the family who would assist her during her stay. What a bold, brave Queen!

When the moment came for her to say goodbye, she didn't fight it. She asked that as many of her children, grandchildren, and great grand's that could be there to stay, sing some of her favorite hymnals, and pray! She told us all to gather around her bed and remember all that she had taught us. She asked us to remember to put God first and hold our heads up because there was nothing to be sad about. She had been blessed and lived a lot longer than she had asked God for. All of her children were saved, and yes, even some of her grandchildren. Unbeknownst to me, she had already had a conversation with Daddy about her time drawing near. He was right by her side, holding her hand, and they kissed each other a few times. She told us she was tired about 15 minutes before leaving us. She simply closed her eyes and took her last breath. I had never experienced anything like that before in my life.

There is so much more in this story, but for now, it's enough. I miss her so much!!! Outside of God himself, she was my everything. I was lovingly called her shadow. We did everything together; even after my marriage, she would always be there with me at all of my doctor appointments because I was such a scared child when it came to needles. I tell you, after she left, everything changed for us all. I couldn't talk to my best friend anymore. She loved us unconditionally, without judgment. For the first time, Daddy began to age. I'll never forget him sitting on the couch alone. His eyes were red and swollen from crying. He said, "When God took her away from me, He took everything!" I sat there and cried with him because, for the first time, my Daddy was so lost. The only enjoyment he seemed to have was his great-granddaughter, Sheila. My daughter. They were like two peas in a pod. Still, it wasn't enough to keep him here. He died of a broken heart (massive heart attack) almost two years to the day of Momma's passing. Mom passed on August 23, 2001, and Dad passed on July 23, 2003. I dream about them often. There are times it's so real that I cry when I wake up and I'm reminded they are not here. I'm grateful to God that I had such a beautiful example of a Proverbs 31 woman!

Thought of the Day

"We make a living by what we get; we make a life by what we give." ~Winston S.Churchill

Who is your example of a Proverbs 31 woman? How do you think she exemplifies these characteristics?

Financial Hardships

Philippians 4:19 ESV

And my God will supply every need of yours according to his riches in glory in Christ Jesus.

Bed
HVAC
Car
Financial Blessing
Food
Job Opportunity

These are just a few of the things I became desperately in need of within the last nine years, post my divorce. When I tell you God has kept me and my two, that's, to say the least. HE'S A KEEPER! I've worked pretty hard to keep my home because it was a stable environment for my children. When we moved to our current location in 2005, it was the only home they knew. They didn't ask for the divorce, and unfortunately, the children tend to take the brunt of it. This is one of the main reasons why their dad and I work together to co-parent and put the children's needs first. Our lives have been our own when it comes to everything else.

Taking care of this home, my car, and any other expected or unexpected needs was my responsibility. When possible, their dad has always done more than his share of making sure the children had what they needed. But, anyone who's a single parent knows that taking care of *one* household is a lot, but taking care of *two* like me (home and a child away from home) was damn near impossible.

For a few years, I slept on a blow-up mattress. My children were growing up fast, especially my son. When he outgrew his bed, I was given another for him by our church family. There were moments my sweet neighbor, Nichelle, would go through her freezer and share a few things with us. There was a moment I'll never forget of her buying bread and lunch meat for us to get through to my next pay period. I know you didn't have a clue (family and friends). I didn't want to become another family member asking for help because a few others seemed to have reached their limit with them. I just didn't bother. Our little family was going through so much. No matter what was going on, the "Prayer of Jabez" was the prayer I taught my children to recite, and we prayed it daily! I posted it everywhere! The bad news during this time was that Nissan Rogue I drove was repossessed. However, the good news at the time was that my daughter was accepted into college at sixteen. She skipped the 11th and 12th grades. This was two years post my divorce. It was a private college and four and a half hours away.

Every year, letters for her were coming to our home while she was in grade school to be a part of all these excellent programs. However, the tuition/fees were so high we couldn't afford it. It was hard to believe that my daughter was headed to college at 16. We, her father and I, knew she was ready. What we had taught her about life, loads of prayer and lots of communication along the way kept us all going. There were loads of trips because she still wasn't driving at this point. My car really went through it. It eventually failed me, and I was donated the use of a 1996 two-door Honda Accord. I learned to live on a fraction of my earnings to make sure she could stay in school and I could take care of the home too.

My friend, Claudia, rode with me to take Sheila to her first day of college. My best friend/big sister, Angela, helped me with food and gas funds throughout that year and beyond. Oh yes, I, too, have had these types of experiences. My friend, Terry, was a sweetheart to let me use her car, which was relatively new to her, to drive to visit and/or pick up my daughter from college for a few months until I could get my next car. Several family members were proud of her but were fearful of her going so far away for college. I learned to trust God. Although I couldn't see how we were going to continue to make it, we did! Sheila stayed on the Dean's List, worked in several positions that built an excellent network for herself in the film industry. With the help of many others outside of her dad and me, she had the opportunity to travel to Prague for two weeks. We were so proud!

During my daughter's last two years of college. I was laid off from my job. I had to let go of the bedroom furniture I was financing. Our HVAC system for my home started to fail us. The bed situation was handled immediately with a blow-up mattress. The job opportunity that saved me was one given by the Goode family, and my HVAC system was repaired several times through my friend Paul whom I've known since 9th grade. He sent a good friend of his to me at a fraction of the cost to help my little family have heat and air when needed. My friend Terry, who allowed me to use her car, later donated her old bedroom furniture.

I couldn't use the frame (I can't remember why), but still, to this day, I have the other pieces and slept on the mattress and box spring until this past August of 2020! My beautiful friend SB (for your protection, sweetie) and I worked on my project. She and I were chatting and started talking about furniture and the need to change some things. We got off course and began to take a look at a particular store—such beautiful furniture. I saw a few beds I liked. She didn't know I hadn't had a bed for several years. She saw several pieces she admired. Immediately she said, let's go! We enjoyed our spontaneous day out. SB found all she needed and then told me that she would help me get the bed I wanted. We worked out a payment arrangement. I was so delighted I cried. I hadn't slept in a bed for a long time. I've paid her in full and will forever be grateful.

God has kept me; he has kept my children! The smile others have seen on my face for the last several years has never been a fake! NEVER! As my mom, Louise, used to say quite often, "It could be worse!". No one, I mean NO

ONE...can tell me my God isn't real! No matter what my family needed, He provided! He's a keeper! We didn't go without food, clothing, shelter, or love! Everything didn't always come when or how I wanted it to come, but He's never left me! I learned that if I just hang in there and be steadfast, he delivers me every time!

Thought of the Day

"At the end of hardship comes happiness."

Korean Proverb

Can you recall a time you went through financial hardship or crisis?

What kept you going, although you couldn't see a way around it?

Grace is...

2 Corinthians 12:9 ESV

But he said to me, "My grace is sufficient for you, for my power is made perfect in weakness." Therefore, I will boast all the more gladly of my weaknesses so that the power of Christ may rest upon me.

God knows our EVERY weakness. Oh yes, even the things you think no one in this world knows. Still, he blesses us amid our mess. What mess do you say? Sometimes it's the thing you know you were taught to never do. Sometimes it's saying things we shouldn't say even when the voice inside your head told you not to before speaking. The mess is sometimes going into places you know you shouldn't, places that tempt you. Often, the mess has been my mindset and making decisions based on how I felt rather than seeking God for the answer. I all my mess, He has NEVER left me, NEVER forsaken me! He's loved me from the moment He created me and sent me soaring to this world through my mother's womb. In all my mess, He's made me still enough to hear His voice. He's hidden all my flaws from those who wanted to use them to hurt me. Even in my weakest moments, He's my power. There's no way that I'd still be here today with hope and love in my heart after all the wrong I've done and all the hurt and pain at times others inflicted.

There are so many great things that have happened to me that I shouldn't have if it were only my weaknesses that God allowed others to see. Some of them are: grandparents that adopted my brother and me to give us a better chance at life, my children, different positions in education that have allowed me to pour into my students, which still allows me to pour into the future, other people who have seen my flaws and they still invest in me and mentor me to assist in me leaving a legacy for my children and generations to come, and very few but powerful lifelong friends that have stood by my side through my darkest and weakest hours to empower me once again to face this world. I'm so grateful!

God's grace, I believe, cannot be earned. There is nothing we can do enough of that even comes close to His love for us. He's already sent His only Son to die for us, knowing all the while we were full of sin. He takes it to an even higher level to cover us and to show up for us even when our actions warrant us to be left standing alone because the situations we get in are so wrong.

There has been so much trauma from all the events this year, 2020. With all the loss we've encountered, still, we can see where God is still blessing us! Don't forget God in this process called life!

Thought of the Day

"I do not at all understand the mystery of grace, only that it meets us where we are but does not leave us where it found us."

Anne Lamott

Can you recall a time you went through financial hardship or crisis?

____

____

____

____

____

What kept you going, although you couldn't see a way around it?

____

____

____

____

Friendship is...

Proverbs 27:17 ESV

Iron sharpens iron, and one man sharpens another.

Have you checked your circle lately? Your associates (business partners, those you work with or network with), you may not be that close to them, but you still spend time with and around them. What about those who you consider your friends? You know the people you spend the majority of your time with, the people you call on when you have fantastic news and devastating news, and the ones you call on when you need a reality check. Webster defines a friend as "one attached to another by affection or esteem. There are a few people that I truly call a friend. I've learned in my 49 years of life that you don't need many. I've learned; there is a big difference in the words friend and comrade/associate. I've defined what a friend is. According to Webster's dictionary, one definition of comrade/associate is "to join together." Just because someone joins you in a particular moment of life doesn't mean they are for you or for your advancement. I've found that they are with you as long as it serves their purpose or plan. When the Word says "iron sharpens iron," I think of a blog called God's Chemistry Set because I love their description of the process:

Sharpening is done by grinding away material on the tool with another abrasive substance harder than the tool itself. This is sometimes followed by polishing the sharp surface, increasing smoothness and correcting small mechanical deformations without regrinding.

I love this description because we immediately see that to be sharpened to become the person God intends you to be, you should ensure you have people in your circle that will demand nothing but your best. At times, I would dare to say they need to be people who have already reached a level in life you aspire to reach. But do we really do that? I have to be honest; in my lifetime, I had to grow into that. I used to simply stick with those who have had the same struggles I had, those who would co-sign on the mess I allowed into my life, and those who I had known for several years. I thought that meant something to everyone, but I found out differently. Instead of friends, I discovered the hard way that some were simply comrades or associates. They were friends of convenience. Meaning, if the cause or situation benefited them in any form or fashion, they were all in until their needs were met. Moving on to the next person was just a continuous cycle of life for them. This was definitely not the best way for me to choose my friends.

As I've gotten older, I've begun to take a real long look at my life. What have I accomplished? Where was I going? What did I need to get there? Whose help did I need to get there? I wasn't looking for someone to hand me anything without me having to work for it, I mean, what real connections did I have? I realized my circle of friends and acquaintances weren't as tight as I thought. I'm sure you've heard the phrase "it's not what you know, but who you know." My God, this is so true! At least it is for me.

God opened so many doors for my children and me through people I've known at times for a quick minute versus years. Those who know me and have spent time with me enough to know my real character, especially those that knew me growing up in Light Oak Community in Shelby, NC where they still call men Sandi, know that I really treasure the friendships that I've had for years. It warms my heart because when I hear that nickname, I feel like I'm at home. But there are a few people that I've recently met, within the last few months to a year or so, who have stretched me and helped me grow far beyond what I thought I could do. Their impact on my life reaches the depths of my soul, causing me to make sure that what I give to myself and others is always the best of me.

The length of time you've spent with someone isn't the determining factor when rating friendships. For me, it's whether or not the relationship is meaningful, purposeful, and both parties benefit from it. I know, it doesn't always work out that way. The moment you realize it, even if it's you who's doing all the talking and not contributing, if the relationship truly has meaning to you, you need to do all you can to own up to that and make the necessary repairs.

Iron sharpening iron is also when a true friend tells you what you don't want to hear. Understand, their chastisement is meant not to hurt you; it's because they love you. A true friend wants to see you at your best and living your best life. They are the ones that spend much time praying before having the hard conversations. They try to find the words that will not hurt you, but will deliver a message is clear and filled with love.

I've been on both ends of this stick. I have been the friend and the one listening to someone sharing their heart and trying to protect me or to stop me from doing something that they know will hurt me. Check your circle. Check your motive for the relationship. Are you growing? Are you also giving anything in the relationship? Have you grown in this relationship? Do you feel the "iron sharpening iron" process taking place? No, it doesn't feel the best, but it's necessary!

Thought of the Day

"True friendship is like sound health. The value of it is seldom known until it be lost."

Charles Caleb Colton

What does a true friend look like to you?

Have you ever encountered a friend who said something that hurt your feelings, then, found out that that friend was actually protecting you? How did you handle this situation?

If You Build...

***1 Thessalonians 5:11* ESV**

Therefore, encourage one another and build one another up, just as you are doing.

Throughout my life, I've developed quite a few great friendships. When I think of those friendships, one true female friend comes to mind, Angela. We grew up in the same neighborhood, Light Oak Community, lovingly called by those of us who lived there "the LOC"! I first met Angela through her mother, Ms. Margaret, God rest her soul. She was the matriarch of the softball team.

Our house was on a corner lot, and the front of the house faced an open ballfield. Just thinking back on all those awesome afternoons and weekends, the neighborhood kids would go there to play all sorts of games, hopscotch, softball, kickball, etc. brings me joy! This takes me home. I had no clue then that she and I would go through so much together! Some of the best and worst times in my life were shared with her, and I have never regretted it. It didn't matter what the situation was. If I was wrong in the matter, she told me. With love, Angela did her best for me as a friend. Later, we became more like sisters. She has always encouraged me.

It was around the mid to late '90s when our friendship grew stronger. We had an opportunity to work together as educators. My classroom was located right across the hall from hers. It was only my fifth year in education and she took the time to make sure I knew where to find the things I needed and to whom I could take any concerns I had. Angela has always been very resourceful. She made my stay there so enjoyable. We shared so many wonderful school days and adventures. We also began to share our life events. Angela and I have been through everything together. She's had much patience and never judged me as I went through financial struggles, loss of other friendships, loss of a child, loss of parents, divorce, and at times loss of myself. Angela is the big sister I never had. Her words of encouragement and gentle reminders of God's Word have helped me beyond measure. I feel forever indebted to her!

Women encouraging other women is something I feel we need more of. Being reared by my grandmother (Momma), Louise gave me a beautiful glimpse of two generations ahead of me. She made it her business to connect spiritually and to encourage other women. I was her shadow and went everywhere with her.

Momma introduced me to her tribe. She put the women she loved as sisters, daughters, and mentors in my path to help guide me throughout life. Because of these connections, I realized that we as women have our own way of doing things and living life, but we are all connected.

Momma placed women of different ages, different life situations, and different races all around me. Throughout her 70 plus years of life, she had encouraged them to do things many they thought they couldn't. When she passed, the same tribe of women helped me heal and continue this journey called life. Many of them were adopted aunties, mothers, and grandmothers. They helped me with the rearing my own children by giving their time, sharing their own life experiences, and giving advice when needed. I'm forever grateful! Do you realize the many households and families we touch as women encouraging women? Letting another woman know that she isn't alone is very important.

When we reveal our souls in a trusted space to others who have made it through what we're going through, we then begin to heal. To encourage others is divine power. When we can set ourselves aside, and genuinely focus on the another person we can create a healing atmosphere.

There are times that we can be our worst enemy by thinking we aren't qualified for the task God has for us to do. I know, I've been there. Fear of failure and not doing a great job has kept me from doing some wonderful things that would have helped many. I didn't think I was as good as______ or I couldn't do it as well as ______. But God! I believe he has people placed in our path to remind us of who He is and what He has planted deep within us all.

Even today, a single mom who happens to be a parent of one of my students recently lost her job. A horrible snowball effect left her little family without quite a few necessities to keep her household running smoothly. I assisted her and her daughter in accessing her class using a platform that neither of them had the opportunity to learn.

She was extremely frustrated because she knew that her misfortune caused her daughter to fall behind tremendously. I immediately took the educator hat off, and I connected with her as one single mom to another. At that moment, I reminded her to hang in there. The current situation wasn't going to be a permanent one. I asked her to please do all she could to continue to seek new employment. I shared with her that I, too, was a single mom, that I had experienced the exact same struggles along this journey. I heard and felt her pain. I didn't want her to feel alone or defeated! Maybe I wasn't supposed to (as an educator on duty), but I did...I told her I would be praying for her and that she was definitely not alone. It seemed to calm her spirits. She thanked me and stated that she wouldn't give up. Her children needed her. My God, my heart was wide open! Anyone who knows me knows that my two diamonds (we're all April babies) are the only reason why I'm still here before you and had the opportunity to write this book. Had someone not prayed for me or encouraged me, I wouldn't be here. It WAS my children. There are times I wanted to end it all, but when I visualized my children's faces and thought about the impact my death would have on them, I just couldn't do it. I couldn't give up. Through the many tears and heartache, I had to get up and keep it moving. My heart has been blessed with others who have encouraged me on this journey, men and women. As a woman, I feel we could definitely continue to do a better job from one sister to another.

I want to say thank you! Thank you to all the women, family or friends, who've been a part of my life at any time from my birth to and through 49 years. It doesn't matter whether the impact was positive or negative, whether the friendship is a current one or has ended due to my actions or yours. You played some part in my life, and have helped me become the woman I am today. I ask you for forgiveness if the friendship ended due to something I said or did. Truly I do. I also forgive you if our friendship ended due to something you said or did. I can't move forward and live the life God gave me out loud and free without forgiveness. Does it mean we'll all come together and sing Kumbaya? Nah, it's ok. What I've learned is that we all are trying to figure out life daily. We're all in different areas of our lives, and some of us may never be in each other's presence again. Continue to encourage one another no matter what. It goes a long way beyond the person we uplift. Encouragement saves lives. I dare say that it stretches and reaches generations when done genuinely. Know this, I love you, my sister! I wish nothing but God's love, sheer joy, and happiness in your life and all those you touch.

Thought of the Day

"Be anencourager, the world already has enough critics."
Unknown

When was the last time you encouraged someone?

Recall a moment someone encouraged you. How did it make you feel?

The Broken-hearted...

<u>John 15:1-27</u> ESV

"I am the true vine, and my Father is the vinedresser. Every branch in me that does not bear fruit he takes away, and every branch that does bear fruit he prunes, that it may bear more fruit. Already you are clean because of the word that I have spoken to you. Abide in me, and I in you. As the branch

cannot bear fruit by itself, unless it abides in the vine, neither can you, unless you abide in me. I am the vine; you are the branches. Whoever abides in me and I in him, he it is that bears much fruit, for apart from me you can do nothing. ..."

This scripture pierces my heart every time I read it. I immediately think of the many times in life that I've felt alone. Yes, I know I have friends and family (what's left of them). But, aren't we all dealing with life as it is. Why should I complain or whine about whatever is challenging me at the time? In this very moment that I'm writing, I'm heartbroken. I had to end yet another romantic relationship. Every time I think I've got it right, it's always the total opposite.

People are good at sending their representatives. We all want to make the best impressions, yet I believe we should be honest about our true nature. Our real character must be represented at all times. A person should know what they are getting into when it comes to building a relationship with someone. I'm pretty transparent. I've always been that way, and I tend to expect the same with those I come in contact with. That doesn't always happen, hence the breakup.

The last phrase of this scripture, "for apart from me you can do nothing, "... hits me harder than anything. I realize that no matter how simple you think a situation is, even getting into a relationship with another, you'd better include God first. Sometimes, we don't even ask Him if we should even give them time to consider the relationship. We just jump in headfirst without a thought because it appeared to be perfect, only to find it was fool's gold!

With every part of my life these days, I realize I can't do anything alone. Our Father offers you the opportunity to save yourself from a lot of wasted time and energy. However, many of us think we can handle life's challenges on our own. He is the one who knows all about who we are and the road ahead of us. It's like trying to reach a destination we've never been to without GPS assistance or at least speaking to someone who knows the path we need to take.

Our Father asks us to bear fruit. The path we've chosen, is it profiting us anything that uplifts the Kingdom and puts us closer to the life God intended us to have? Every year before my birthday, I tend to go into this phase of mentally taking inventory to see what I have accomplished. must admit, some of those years, physically and spiritually, I've taken several steps backward. I was nowhere near where I should've been spiritually. There are times when I've noticed I've failed the same test at least twice, sometimes three times. I get so frustrated with myself. The self-talk is often brutal. Hindsight is 20/20. I seem to always walk away by saying, "Cassandra, you're smarter than that. All the red flags were there and still you continued the same course." I've been in this space in my mind too many times to count.

"Abide in me, and I in you. As the branch cannot bear fruit by itself, unless it abides in the vine, neither can you, unless you abide in me." I talked to my lifelong friend of 39 years, EP, about some of the things I'd like to have in my next home. I mentioned a prayer room. He said something so profound. He said, "I'm sorry, I need every part of my home to be prayed over." I received that. EP said, "The enemy is on his job 24/7 so why should I not be in continuous prayer?" We talked about how some of us will set aside a time of the day and place to pray or speak to God. We both feel that we can talk to our God at any time and in any place, on the job, in your car, at the store, at an event, it doesn't matter.

My Father says, "abide in me, and I in you." He didn't say at any particular time or in a particular place. He is a keeper. He is THE Keeper! Do you realize the peace you'd have daily if you'd begin to simply pray wherever you are? I we thank God, ask for his mercy and grace when all else fails, ask him to get you to that state of peace when all hell has broken loose or just be a fence around us He will supply all of these things. Center yourself and ask

God to help you learn to be content no matter what state you're in. Do you know the power in that?

More and more each day, I'm making room for Him. I trust Him. He's never left me to deal with anything alone. I was the one who thought I could do it alone or who felt so embarrassed or ashamed at what happened and felt He didn't want such a person in His presence. No! All lies, He loves me, and yes, He loves you too! He's always there!

Thought of the Day

"The best way to heal from a broken heart is to give God all of the pieces."

Unknown

What life experience left you broken hearted?

____

____

____

____

____

What steps have you taken to heal?

____

____

____

____

Judge Not...

<u>*Galatians 6:1*</u> *ESV*

Brothers, if anyone is caught in any transgression, you spiritual should restore him in a spirit of gentleness. Keep watch on yourself, lest you too be tempted.

As a teen, footloose and fancy-free, I still had much to learn. I remember hearing life stories of family members of both sides and friends of the family. The things said and done concerning how they handled their life challenges weren't what I thought the best way. What did I know? Yes, I was saved at an early age (7 years old), and I was indeed His soldier! Umm chile! As the years went by, and I lived a bit longer, I began to face similar challenges and decisions. It's different when it's YOU!

Why is it that we can be quick to judge others in their moments of weakness? We look for what's wrong rather than what is done well. Professionally or personally, we all have our ways and beliefs about how things should be done. We may have a better way of doing things, but it's not always the only way. Some of us have done well with living our lives in the shadows, knowing full well that if the light was shed on our situation, we would possibly lose everything. It's comfortable, and you get some type of joy out of it. But it's ok, it's YOUR life, right? NO! It's not ok!!! I know, trust me, we don't like being called out. We don't like to be told we are wrong even when we know at times it's done out of love. There's the feeling of guilt, embarrassment, and shame. I've been there.

Momma (grandmother Louise) was my first introduction to God's love and grace. She handled all my transgressions with the utmost care. Don't get me wrong, she didn't excuse it, nor did she spare me the knowledge of how deeply hurt she was about whatever it was that happened. Momma had a way of getting you straight and still showing you love all at the same time. As a young adult and on into adulthood, Momma would sit me down and ask what was REALLY going on. She knew what the truth was before asking, but she wanted to hear it from me. She wanted to see what my thought process was. Why did I make the choice I made? No matter how I justified it, if I was wrong, she would tell me. She would also do her best to show me where I went wrong. Sometimes it hurt, and I would get upset about it. Momma would say, "You may not want to talk to me right now, but I love you. I'd rather correct you than you pay a larger price for the wrong you did later."

God has a way of placing people in our lives that has our best interest at heart. It may not always be family. It could be a colleague, friend, or someone you have known for a short while. Just as hard as it is for you to take the criticism, it's even harder for someone to know they must say something that could hurt your feelings, risk the loss of friendship or relationship, or at the very least it alters the relationship so much so that the communication is not the same. But they must do it; the Word says so. I've been on both ends of the situation, and it's tough to be the one correcting your loved one.

Nevertheless, you don't want to see your loved one hurt or going down a path that could also hurt others. If the love you have between you is real, it will stand the test of time. Yes, it may be a bit awkward for a while, but the relationship will be ok in the end.

Having others look to me for spiritual guidance and being responsible for helping someone else through their transgressions sometimes seems to be a bit more than I can handle. I realize I'm not perfect, and Lord knows the choices I've made in my life have proven that. But God! I've learned a lot from those choices that have cost me a price several wouldn't be willing to pay. Only the grace of God kept me. There are times I've felt so damaged and unworthy, I wanted to let go of life. Fortunately, I loved my children too much to put them through that type of pain.

I've had to practice this scripture several times with my children. At times, my heart has been ripped out, trying to look past choices they made that made me, as parent, feel responsible. I was reminded by others that my children have been blessed by God to have free will too. At a certain age, they know right from wrong. They have been given the tools and support to be successful and to flourish. Still, they may make choices that they know are wrong and not think about all it will cost them in the end. I'm transparent with my children. As they get older and begin to go through certain things in life, I've shared my truth, letting them know of my own transgressions.

I know some people feel a parent shouldn't do that because the child could use it against them to do what they want. My belief is, look at my life, see what it cost me. Learn from my mistakes and try to avoid the same trap. If then they chose the wrong path anyway, I can't be held accountable at that point. I've warned you and given you the outcome. Is that easy to do? NO! I've spent days just sick, crying, and not sleeping well because I want my children to experience the life God has for them. I don't want to lose them to this cruel world we live in. There are people among us that allow the enemy to use them for the demise of others. The hardest thing to do is to watch your children make choices that they will pay dearly for. Although I birthed them, I'm learning they belong to God, and He has a path and a plan of His own for them. I must remember that in all I do to parent them. My children being 24 and 16, are at a point where now I can only guide them. There are some really tough conversations. Some leave them crying, some leave me crying...sometimes we're both crying. But, God has directed us to do so.

Those of us who are spiritual, those who believe in His word, are to restore those caught in transgression. He didn't say those that are perfect. How do you help or lead someone through something you've never experienced?

You can't begin to know the pain and frustration they are going through. We, as His children, as believers, must do all we can to help steer our brother or sister back to the path that God has for them. We should at least try. Don't hesitate, let go of thinking it's about you. The life you are living is for His glory. Let His love take over your heart to help your brother or sister. It will be worth it for your sake and theirs.

Thought of the Day

Don't give up what you want most for what you want now.

Unknown

If part of where temptation comes from is in our heart, what are some things you can do to protect yourself from it (temptation)?

Spiritually & Emotionally Fit...

Proverbs 31:17 *ESV*

She dresses herself with strength and makes her arms strong.

Ladies, how many of us want those Michelle Obama arms. Honey! She's beautiful inside and out! But, when I read this scripture, I see more than just our physical appearance being called to attention. I see the strength of a woman and the hats we figuratively wear! I swear, I want to take some of them off and burn them. With the many hats we wear, we must definitely stay physically and spiritually fit. Here are a few of the hats most of us wear:
Sister
Auntie
Wife
Mother, doctor, lawyer, psychologist, etc.
Boss
Colleague
Volunteer
Friend
Life Coach
Shero

Many times, this journey has taken its toll on me. There were times when I wasn't sure which hat to wear and in which season I should wear each hat. Unfortunately, sometimes they were worn out of season.

Momma, Louise Lockhart Gill was a hat-wearing sister! Nobody wore a hat like her! I have to say her name like that because Momma taught us to be respectful of our elders, and she used to tell me, "Girl put a handle (respect)on my name!

Anyone who knew her well knew she had a hat for every season and every event or outfit. I was blessed to go shopping with her every weekend. It was one of her favorite things to do. I have fond memories of the time and money spent going to some of the most expensive places to find wonderful treasures. She exuded such class and grace at all times, however, when the right hat was placed on her head to complete the look she wanted, you couldn't tell that sister anything! I loved watching her. When Momma was in her element; she was confident and fierce. It was equivalent to her putting on her cape. She was my "Shero" for sure! I knew her true nature, her character. Talk about dressing yourself in strength! She clothed herself in strength strong enough to face all that life throws at us. Whew, what a testimony!

She wore all of the different hats (roles) mentioned, and she wore them well. Even with tears in her eyes, she would straighten that hat out and keep it moving. Through Momma and the trauma our family experienced in losing my mother, Sheila, I was still allowed to experience two generations of strength. I've carried that strength with me throughout my life.

At 49, I'm still learning how and when to wear each hat. It helps to think back to all of the memories shared with Momma and how I watched her effortlessly remove one hat and put on another. In every role, God gave me a front-row seat. Momma and her strength starred in every scene and scenario.

My Momma wasn't just a momma. She was also a sister. I remember visiting her siblings as a child. We visited her brothers James Lockhart, Sr. (aka Black Jesus) and Roosevelt Lockhart. Those two were something! I also remember my Great Uncle James. He was a strong union man who had left the south and did well up north.

I learned more about him when he retired and returned to the south. He was hilarious and always kept a joke or two on hand. He would recall and share some of the funniest childhood and family events in such a way that you felt as if you were there! Momma looked to him for business advice. There were days she'd go over to his home to sit and listen to gospel music. This, too, was a way for them to minister. I loved it. We'd sing and praise God together during all the world's challenges. Uncle James passed away a month later. It was somewhat the same with my Great Uncle Roosevelt (her younger brother).

We love gospel music (preferably quartets & mass choirs). Uncle Roosevelt was also an excellent cook. Uncle Roosevelt had had a stroke some years ago so Momma would check on him often. He was the only person on earth who called me Candy. I miss him so much! He used to send me care packages of food for college all the time. Once, Momma went for a visit alone. She was checking on him as she usually did. She found him in his special place, the kitchen, unresponsive. It shook her world.

Momma also had a sister, Great Aunt Willie Mae Lloyd and a double first cousin that reared with her like a sister, Great Aunt Lenora Allison. They were all very close and some hat-wearing sisters. They all wore their hats, physically and figuratively, with their own flair.

My Aunt Willie Mae's birthday and mine were only a day apart, hers was a day after mine. For years when I was small, Momma celebrated my birthday a day late. She kept her sister's birthday so close to her heart that she didn't realize mine preceded hers.

Aunt Willie Mae could sing and was known to breed dogs. Aunt Lenora was a great cook! I loved her Red Velvet cakes. Momma and Aunt Lenora could have passed for twins. After Momma died, I loved s her Aunt Lenora as often as possible because it was like seeing Momma again. Man! Those sisters were close. They had all suffered quite a bit. Momma and Aunt Lenora both had gone through losing a child.

When they got together collectively or one on one, they shared their blessings, and they shared their latest challenges. They cried, prayed, and laughed together for many years. One of the last memories I have of Aunt Lenora was visiting her after she had battled cancer. She was bouncing back at the time and had enough strength to cook us a meal. It was delicious as always. She kept the laughs and food coming. You never visited any of the Young, Lockhart, and Linder family without having a meal. They believed in breaking bread together and sharing in the love of family. Aunt Lenora was the last one to pass. I miss them all so much.

Considering what happened to my birth mother, God could not have given my brother and me a better mom than Momma. Through all the hurt and pain, the sacrifices of her own time, money, love, etc., she always gave us her best. She didn't have to do it. Many others wanted to help, but she refused. As a mother, she wanted all she had left of her daughter to be within her reach and a part of her legacy. I'm forever grateful.

As a wife, she spent fifty-one years with Daddy. She spoiled him rotten. He didn't care to eat other people's cooking or go out to eat much. No one knew him as she did! Momma ran a tight ship at home, and although she's not with us, her house rules still stand. Even as she prepared for her death, she took the time to prepare him as best she could to let go.

I've been told that Momma spent weeks before her death talking to Daddy about her departure. It had to be the hardest thing ever, knowing that all you've ever known was each other. They had loved each other, shared children and the loss of children. Together, they had experienced the birth of grandchildren and great-grandchildren. They had spent a lifetime together. Fifty-one years together ended in a few moments. They shared a kiss and held hands moments before she took her last breath. The strength she had was unexplainable. She would often say if it wasn't for God, she wouldn't have made it. My grandfather died of a broken heart almost two years to the date of Momma's passing.

I think my birth mother, Sheila, and the strength she displayed. As I stated earlier, she suffered tremendous verbal and physical abuse simply because someone looked her way, spoke to her, or was kind to her. Dealing with that on a daily basis took an enormous amount of strength. I can't imagine the way it made her feel.

As a teenager, I remember going through those awkward stages and thoughts of are you good enough or I pretty enough. At times during that stage, girls can be the worst! They tease you and talk about what you look like, what you're wearing, and how smart you are. Couple that with the fact that she had an abusive boyfriend at fifteen, had me at sixteen, and then married at some point at an age that required parental consent. Then she had my brother at seventeen.

I was told she ended up depressed, and although she cared for us, she let herself go. She made the hard decision to leave my father and protect us. This was a bold move because my father had told her that he would kill her if she ever left him. She knew that what he said was true because he had come close to keeping that promise many times.

We, my brother and I, were the only extensions of her outside of her family. She took the chance of saving us all and went back home. Although she took that chance and still lost her life in front of me, she gathered enough strength for her last words to be the word, Jesus! There was nothing more she could do, even though I was right there in front of her and my brother just a few feet away in another room; she knew only the strength of Jesus could protect us and keep us safe as she left us.

In life's challenging moments, you may feel that you are not enough, or you that you can't go on. You may feel that you do not have the strength to fulfil the story God has written for you. Remember that others learn from your journey! Believe it or not, YOU are someone's SHERO or HERO! Take the strength God has offered you and get ready to leave a legacy greater than you ever dreamed it would be!

Thought of the Day

"Better is the enemy of best"

Sam Beechum

Do you live a life that you don't love because you are worried about what others will think about you?

Do you quit when the going gets tough? Why or why not?

Mental Health & Wellness...

John 16:33 ESV

I have said these things to you, that in me you may have peace. In the world, you will have tribulation. But take heart; I have overcome the world."

How is it that I, at age three, and many other children who are left behind for any reason; death, jail, addictions, or simply abandoned, find peace? How is it that mothers and fathers of murdered children or children who have passed way too soon to find peace? In this world, riddled with hatred and no thought of the consequences of our actions, where do we go to find peace?

I know the feeling of pain as a child left behind. There was no way for me to truly grasp what had happened at such an early age. I believed that when my mother woke up she would come to get me. For many years, I had nightmares about someone chasing me, trying to hurt me or trying to kill me. This played on repeat in my mind for a very long time. There were times I'd share my dreams, and Momma would ask me, "Who have you been talking to?" As I described to her what was happening, she realized the dreams I was having weren't just a nightmare. She discovered it was the life I lived.

We'd lived as a family victimized by domestic violence. Momma often mentioned that she wished that African American families were open to more than just praying to get through all the pain they had experienced. Counseling or seeing a therapist should have been the next step immediately when she lost my Uncle Joe Louis, a Marine, to the Vietnam War in his early twenties and then my mother at the tender age of nineteen.

The pain of watching a mother and father suffer the pain of losing their children was more than I can understand. Yet, I watched this unbearable real-life story unfold. It took me giving birth to my children Sheila and Sidney to even begin to feel the depths of Momma's and Daddy's pain. Just the thought of anything happening to them brings me to tears, and my heart aches horribly. I honestly pray out loud every time. No Lord, I refuse to accept it! Please protect them no matter where they are, no matter what they are doing. Please, protect them!

Those of us who have experienced a profound loss of any sort know that you never get over it. You find a way, eventually, to live with it. My grandparents found a way to celebrate their three remaining children. no matter the occasion or age! Momma would always cook our favorite meals and our favorite cakes during our special days and holidays. It brought her so much joy! But, when everyone was gone and back to their daily routine, I'd find her praying on her knees aloud. Most of the time, she was brought to tears praying for her babies that were alive and asking God to help her move on with her life as she unbearably missed the two babies taken from her in such tragic ways.

Momma's way of finding peace was exemplified in her relationship with her Heavenly Father. During every birthday, family event, and the anniversaries of the deaths her two children, she was really quiet and deep in thought. I saw her silently wiping away tears for years. It never failed. I'd watch the calendar just to find a way to brighten her day when those moments came around.

Momma sharing Christ's story and the Prayer of Salvation with me so long ago is the gift that has kept giving long after her passing. I didn't realize the strength and true peace it would give me until I experienced my own loss and pain challenges. Since their death, I've had to go through counseling at least three times. Outside of God, Momma was the only person I felt I could genuinely trust. She was the only person I knew would continue to love me without judgment. As stated before, she would let you know when you were wrong. But, she NEVER judged you. When I became an adult, she would do all she could to show me how to correct the behavior and left the judgment up to God. This gave me peace when some of those I thought loved me, family and friends, judged me harshly and treated me differently.

After Momma's and Daddy's death, I learned to lean heavily on God's Word. I realized that he would never leave me nor forsake me. It was all I felt I had left. To this day, some hold my past against me. God's love and all the promises He's kept have proven to be more than enough for me! He has given me the gift of loyal friends and deeper family connections that thrive beyond the hurt and pain.

If you too want to know the peace within that Momma shared with me, here's a Sinner's Prayer according to Billy Graham; my maternal great-grandmother Mary Miller loved him.

Dear Lord Jesus, I know that I am a sinner, and I ask for Your forgiveness. I believe You died for my sins and rose from the dead. I turn from my sins and invite You to come into my heart and life. I want to trust and follow You as my Lord and Savior. In Your Name. Amen.

Thought of the Day

"No matter what the day brings and no matter how hard life hits you, if you can breathe, smile and keep moving on! Once you have life, know that God is alive!"

Ernest Agyemang Yeboah

When things go wrong, what is your go-to solution and why?

'Tis So Sweet...

<u>Ephesians 2:8-9</u> ESV

For by grace, you have been saved through faith. And this is not your own doing; it is the gift of God, not a result of works, so that no one may boast.

Good God, Almighty! Is there even a way to count how many times God's grace saved me? It's endless! How many times have you caught yourself failing? It wasn't planned that way but yet again, there you were! What does God do? He never leaves you. He stands there with arms open wide. He doesn't say, "I told you so," like others would gladly say.

Just imagine you were told as Jesus was that you must die to offer the world true freedom. You are the one and only person that could save the world. Now, imagine that the very people you were sent to save, turned their backs on you, ridiculed you and sentenced you to death.

We can never truly understand what Jesus went through to give us the opportunities we have. The love that He has for us supersedes understanding. However, He continues to extend it to us when we are at our worse.

Growing up without my parents was difficult. Knowing that my father had killed my mother was not only painful but it shaped the way I looked at myself, my family and my world. How could I not believe that little bit of the evil that lived in my father hadn't been placed in me? I had his DNA! How were my Momma and Daddy able to look at my brother and myself and not see the man who had stolen the life of their daughter? How could the give us so much love through their loss and pain? I other wondered how my Momma could love God so much even though He had allowed unimaginable pain into her life. But, she did. She was committed to serving a God she believed knew all things. She was committed to believing that all things worked together for the good of those who loved and served Him. She walked by faith and her commitment was much more than words spoken in public places. In private, she communed with God. She had an intimate relationship that went well beyond the walls of a church or the eyes of a community. My Momma was a true woman of God. She led by example. Although I have made many missteps, nothing was a mistake. I have the same faith in God that Momma had. She taught me to pray without ceasing. I still do that. She taught me to believe without wavering. I still do that. She taught me to trust that He will always be there for me. I believe that with my whole being. God is faithful, loving and true. I know that no matter what I do, where I go or how far I drift away from Him, I can always come home. I knew that when Momma and Daddy were with me. Because of them, I know that I always have a home with my Heavenly Father.

<u>Romans 12:2</u> ESV

Do not be conformed to this world, but be transformed by the renewal of your mind, that by testing you may discern what is the will of God, what is good and acceptable and perfect.

To be "transformed by the renewal of your mind" calls for some serious reprogramming of the mind. I understand it to mean you have to change your mindset as you navigate through the world we live in. It is not changing yourself in the human form, but changing as a spiritual being while you live in a natural body. That body is only a vessel that hosts your soul. Merriam-Webster Dictionary has at least three definitions of transform. The one that is most relevant to this piece is "to change in character or condition."

Take the time to pause for about five solid minutes and think about where you allow your mind to go. I know some of us have no clue how crazy, filthy, or damaging our thoughts can be. Maybe it's just me, but I know for sure it seems easier to think of all that's wrong before I think of all that's good and perfect in His eyes. I find myself often saying, no, Cassandra, think positively. The more I caught myself saying this, the more I realized what I feed my mind automatically oozes out into my life.

Sometimes, we desperately need the right thought to come forth. If not, we find ourselves floundering. I believe that we were born in sin. Thus, God has to remind us to "renew" our minds consistently! If the human side of us was aligned with the spiritual part of us and walking together in harmony, we wouldn't have to reprogram our minds to think as God would have us to think.

To discern is defined by Merriam-Webster as "to come to know or recognize mentally." I would go even further to say discernment is to know spiritually. It's something I pray for. You may be shocked by the motives people have for being a part of your life. In fact, you may be shocked by life, itself! What I've learned about discernment thus far is to watch what people do, as opposed to what they say. You may call it a gut feeling or a red flag. Sometimes, I've called it a vibe that just doesn't sit well with me. There are times I went with my heart, although my head said something totally different. I paid dearly for those mistakes. Things that were definitely not of God, led me far away from the path that God had planned for me. I had many sleepless nights, so much loss, and so many tears. Some friends walked away never to return. God seemed to call out to me so loud, and still, I tried to hide due to all that had taken place in my life. I knew much of it wasn't right in His eyes. I felt I wasn't good, acceptable, or perfect enough for Him. However, He didn't walk away from me. As I said earlier, I wanted to let go of life a few times, but my children's love kept me here. I knew it wasn't fair to them and it wouldn't have been fair to God either!

Reading God's word and prayer has given me the tools to renew my mind, ensuring I seek God's will, not my own. Can you imagine what our lives would be like if God treated us like man does? We can be so harsh with each other. No matter what we do, God still loves us. To come close to being able to offer that kind of love to others, we must stay in tune with Him.

How can we come to discern what is good, acceptable, and perfect like Him? Just as we would with our closest friend, we must spend time with Him. Think of a person you know who has your back no matter what. They don't condone your wrongdoing, but they are there for you when you truly need them. No, you may not speak as often as you should some days. But, they are the person you've spent time with enough to know they have your best interest at heart. They want the best for you. Well, get this! God has already done so much more for you. He loves you like none other. When I stop and think about the fact that He gave His one and only Son to save us from our sins, I know I couldn't do the same.

Prayer is my way of staying close to God. We talk several times a day. I don't wait for a set time of the day to connect with Him. He's available 24/7. I can't tell you how good that makes me feel. There are times when things happen, and I can't sleep or get my thoughts together. He's right there! There is no way to know God's will and what He considers to be excellent and acceptable without spending time and talking to Him daily.

Thought of the Day

"The renewed mind is the canvas on which the spirit of God can paint."

Bill Johnson

What are the areas of defeated thinking in your mind?

The Family

Sheila Gill-Farmer
My Mother

Edward and Louise Gill
My Grandparents

Freddie L. Farmer Jr.
My Brother

Sheila Pauline Smith -My Daughter
Sidney Elijah Smith- My Son

Be Anxious For Nothing...

Philippians 4:6 ESV

Do not be anxious about anything, but in everything by prayer and supplication with thanksgiving let your requests be made known to God.

Growing up with my grandparents was a blessing. I experienced things from their generation that I don't think most of my generation was privy to. Momma and Daddy grew up in the 1920s through the 1940s.

Momma was reared by my great-great-grandmother; her mother died when she was around five years old. Their way of life, values, and morals were influenced by generations ahead of them. Things like sex and marriage (not just getting married, but how to stay married) weren't popular conversations. How to be a lady, dress, take care of the home, speak when in public, cook, etc. were important things that were passed down from generation to generation.

In her time, little girls were to be in the company of their mothers and grandmothers, for the most part, to learn these things by watching and participating. You rarely see that now. No, it wasn't all I should've learned, but it's all she had to give me. I grew to love her even more for all she taught me. It's funny, but I didn't truly understand it all until later.

Momma was a private nurse for a wealth family. The woman of the house, Julia, grew to love me like her own. Julia introduced me to so many things I would've never experienced. We weren't poor, but we didn't have the financial means to enjoy some of the opportunities wealth brings.

Because she trusted her and knew I was safe, my grandmother allowed us to have our own relationship. Julia became like an adopted mother after I lost my godmother, Thelma Littlejohn. My Godmother had sass, class, and was gorgeous from the inside out. She loved her children as well as my brother and me. I miss her. She died of leukemia when I was in middle school, I believe.

My grandmother introduced me to and placed women of all walks of life. She selected those she knew would love me like their own and teach me all they could from their own experiences. Most of them had gotten married at an early age. Because of this, I looked at getting married beyond my twenties as marrying late.

Growing up, my cousins and I used to think thirty was old. At forty-nine, I know differently. Being married was glorified as something that made you a proper woman. Back then and sometimes now, a woman without a husband was looked at as if something was wrong with her. You were considered an old maid if you were single beyond the age of twenty-five.

As teen girls, we used to draw hearts, placing our names and the name of the guys we were dating inside. It symbolized that we would never part. Sometimes, we would write our names with the guy's last name attached as if we were already married. My grandparents knew that I was growing up, but all that was said was, "Don't be a fast girl! You shouldn't be anywhere talking to a boy alone. Don't have sex at all until you're married, and if you do and you get pregnant he should make a proper woman out of you!" Marriage was believed to keep other people from degrading you or treating you like an outcast.

My grandfather didn't have it in him to sit me down and have a father-daughter talk about the games men play. (I know, women play them now too, but this is about me. Stay focused, lol). He wasn't taught to do those types of things. He didn't grow up with his parents teaching those types of lessons. Again, he could only give me what he had inside to give. So, he did all he could to run the guys off that liked me. That was his way of protecting me and letting me know he loved me enough not to allow me to be used or mistreated.

I knew nothing about what real love between a young lady and a young man was supposed to look or feel like. I loved the idea of being loved, getting married, and living happily ever after. That's what was always displayed on television, in church, and at times, in front of family and friends. No one sat me down and told me about all the challenges that some couples face nor how to handle them when they come. I believe they felt these conversations were only appropriate once you were grown and married. Unfortunately, this is knowledge that I believe should be taught before one even considers marriage. I've learned marriage is not for everyone!

Momma didn't like me calling a boy my boyfriend. She preferred me to say "my friend." I hated that because all the other guys I didn't spend time with were just my friends. Still, as simple as it was, I should've stuck with that. Quite a few of the guys I dated should've remained "friends". No shade. I've found myself to be one that always gave far too much of myself emotionally and physically before they ever proved themselves worthy of such.

Needless to say, I was definitely not prepared for marriage at twenty-two. I thought I was. We dated while in college, but we were in two different locations. I was in Winston-Salem, NC, and he was at home, two hours away. Although not too far away, we were only around each other about once a month. He was three years older and we got engaged in my junior year. Several of my friends, male and female, asked me if I was ready for marriage.

I thought I was because I believed we loved each other, and that's all we needed, right? They asked what about all the things I hadn't done yet; travel, live on my own, date other young men. They also inquired about what I wanted to do on my own... for myself. My reply to everyone was that I could do whatever I wanted to do as an individual, as a part of a couple. I believed that. Simple, right?

Remember, conversations about many things that should've been talked about were not talked about at all. We did marriage counseling and talked mostly about being equally yoked, as in the same religious beliefs and a bit about finances, but that was it. It was all done in a day. It was not ongoing or any more in-depth than what you'd ask to talk about.

In our households, we were taught that you didn't tell people outside of your family anything about yourself or your family and we didn't. As with most African Americans at the time, we didn't understand the need for therapy or counseling. To do so was to admit you were crazy and something was definitely wrong. Of course, there was! We both had faced so much loss and pain. Some I knew about and some I didn't. I know that there were many things not talked about or dealt with. Most were avoided to keep from hurting family members and family friends. The truth is, it seems to cause even more hurt and pain once you realize you were kept in the dark and/or specific decisions were made by those that didn't know the truth that made things worse.

In my ex's absence, I will not share certain things. We both brought our own challenges, family influences, and views of what we thought marriage was supposed to look like. I was twenty-two, he was twenty-five and we were both anxious to get married. I couldn't wait to see the beautiful wedding I planned, during my senior year of college, materialize. I was excited about the idea of living with the man with whom I had been physically intimate. I know I was supposed to wait for marriage but I didn't. This would make it right. I missed him! Remember, we only saw each other about once or at most twice a month now that I had a car and was away in college the entire time we dated.

I had never lived on my own. I was going from my grandparents' house to our new little home. I was happy to get to be with him every day! Now that he was my husband, we could do whatever we liked. The way we grew up and our life experiences were very different. We should have sat down and openly talked about some things while we were dating. We should've been gathering data, but we didn't. We had parents and family that we knew loved us. Still, we were unprepared. Please know, there's no blame here! I know that I was wrapped up in the thought of being in love, being a wife, and finally having children! I could hardly think of anything else.

I had a relative who wanted to talk to me about a few things before marriage, but saw how happy I seemed to be and didn't want to ruin it. I told that relative I wish we had had that talk. I deeply respected this family member, and I would have at least considered taking more time to see if I was truly prepared. After the beautiful wedding we had planned and finally settled into a home, I felt everything else would fall into place. It did not.

There was so much that we didn't know about what is needed to have a successful marriage. Things like family influences, morals and values can make or break a relationship. What may be natural and normal for you may not be for your spouse. Conversations about finances, what part each spouse is responsible to handle, are important and should be had prior to saying "I do".

Couples should ask themselves for what purpose did they get married. What is the purpose of the union besides having the title and guiltless sex? What are your spiritual goals? Will there be children and what are your parenting beliefs and strategies? How often will you go on vacation? These are just a few things that we should've talked about before marriage. We should have come to some common ground, and if not, we shouldn't have gotten married. When it's said that hindsight is 20/20, I'm sure my ex-husband and I could both say that so true.

When you can't truly communicate with each other or agree on the most basic things, it could cost you everything! Our little family suffered quite a bit. If we had gotten ourselves together spiritually, consulted God in all we did before making a move, and followed His will instead of our own, I believe we could've made it. There were things I felt we needed more of: open communication about ourselves (past and future), financial check-ins (where do we stand, what do we need to cover, what do we have left, how do we make our money make more money, should we have one pot or one-pot together and several others to reach our goal), vacation (I yearned to have time away from all we went through each year, was willing to always pay my part to help but there were different beliefs on how we could do that and we just couldn't find common ground), the time and attention of my spouse (especially after the birth of my first child, my timing I'm sure wasn't always the best), continue having scheduled date nights as we did before marriage, etc. Did I bore you already? Do you feel the list is too long? I swore when I was in the marriage, it didn't seem so. It meant everything to me. It was essential.

Several years went by. We took each other for granted. Certain things were done out of obligation but not with the intent to ensure it brought joy to each other. We didn't talk much, make solid plans, or dream together anymore. Our lives became about working and paying the bills. We did just enough to keep going. We took no time away from it all, no time to retreat and ensure our marriage was intact.

I'm very ambitious and a diehard planner. I have the mindset and effort to reach my goals. I wanted us to dream, plan, and grow together. I'm sure he had dreams and plans of his own but I can't speak for him, nor will I try. I'm just sharing what I felt during this time. I felt alone and unheard in the marriage. To suggest that I wanted more seemed to make him feel I wasn't happy with what was provided.

We disagreed a lot and I didn't understand why we couldn’t be more, do more, and enjoy more, especially since I wasn't a stay at home wife/mother. I worked too. At the time, I didn't make as much as he did, but I gave my all with what I earned. We seemed to grow further apart. The time and attention of others seemed to validate me. The operative word is "seemed". The grass does look greener on the other side. But, if you water your own grass, you find that your grass can be just as green. If you and your partner work together as one you can create something incredibly beautiful.

There were things done on both sides that didn't help matters. We both made mistakes. A few years later, he became ill. Suddenly, I had to carry my entire family both financially, outside of his disability payments, and emotionally. I felt my life had come to a huge halt. Although I was still alive, I was dying inside. This was new to me because no one in my immediate family had experienced this type of challenge. I was left with no one to talk to other than God. I felt that I had disappointed God already with the spiritual challenges I was dealing with. I gave in to the enemy's advances. I began to go places I had no business going and doing things I knew better than to do!

When you rush into anything without ensuring you have all the information, or you don't talk freely and openly without judgment no matter how much it hurts, it sets you up for failure. In marriage or any other serious relationship, you must be brutally honest. What many of us fail to realize is that the decisions we make don't only affect us, they affect everyone connected to us, negatively or positively. Be sure to slow down and take your time. Pray and ask God is this for you. Are you ready? If not, ask him for patience and wisdom to make the right decision. If you fail to do this, the price you pay may be far more than you can live with. Trust me, I know. I wasn't expecting to share all this in the book. I will hold some details between me and those affected by my decisions to not further inflict our wounds that have finally begun to heal. I was encouraged to share this much because I can't "pour from a dirty bucket" as a life coach. I must cleanse myself first in hopes of helping many others purge. I know, it opens me up for more judgment. But, remember, a man can't place me in heaven or hell. Only God has that power. I'm so grateful because he has forgiven me, and He will forgive you too! With a pure heart, learning from your past, never returning to your sin, and giving Him all you are, the good, the bad, the ugly He is faithful to forgive and restore you!

Thought of the Day

"Our anxiety does not come from thinking about the future, but from wanting to control it.

Kahlil Gibron

What do you have in your life right now that makes you feel thankful?

THE REST...

Psalm 15

1 Lord, who shall abide in thy tabernacle? who shall dwell in thy holy hill?

2 He that walketh uprightly, and worketh righteousness, and speaketh the truth in his heart.

3 He that backbiteth not with his tongue, nor doeth evil to his neighbour, nor taketh up a reproach against his neighbour.

4 In whose eyes a vile person is contemned; but he honoureth them that fear the Lord. He that sweareth to his own hurt, and changeth not.

5 He that putteth not out his money to usury, nor taketh reward against the innocent. He that doeth these things shall never be moved.

I was like most girls at my age. I was twenty-two but not quite a grown woman. I had this fairytale story in my head of being in love every day, working and making money together, making purchases together or for each other, having babies, and lots of travel and vacationing together. I saw us moving up the corporate ladder and moving out of our little home into a much larger one after five years.

Nothing went the way I thought it should. I thought we'd still date once we were married. I guess my ex-husband went into survival mode because anything close to dating and going out regularly ended with marriage and he continued this line of thinking most of it.

I wanted us to go on a vacation on our anniversary. I am a teacher, so every summer, most of my colleagues would vacation several places before returning to school in the fall. My ex and I didn't go anywhere. I thought he'd plan something special but he didn't. We talked about going to the Biltmore Estate. I wanted to spend the weekend in Asheville, we did not. I wanted to buy a meal there at the estate. We did not. We had to pack sandwiches and drinks in a cooler. We BOTH were working, and I just didn't understand why we couldn't enjoy ourselves this one time out of the year. We toured the estate, ate those sandwiches, and drove our black a's right back home. I loved seeing the estate but was so disappointed that we didn't at least stay overnight in Asheville.

The following year we went to Charleston. I believe we had an overnight stay, I can't remember. I do know we took a van tour, which was nice. I think we drove out to see the Gula people. I have several in my family on my father's side. We saw a few stores on that side of SC, but that's it. I remember smelling the seafood, OMG!!! I was so hungry! I think it was this trip or the next one to Hilton Head for a weekend where we enjoyed a weekend stay right by the beach. We didn't have an oceanfront view, but the hotel was stunning. I know that in Charleston, I stayed in the bathroom and couldn't eat enough. Had no clue, but I was five weeks pregnant!

Needless to say, my pregnancy was the best thing that happened in our first two years of our marriage. Having a new life growing inside of you is truly a God-given gift. It was the most beautiful experience. Even when my pain was at its worst, when I gained weight, found myself exhausted, and made loads of trips to the potty because of nausea, I lived for this moment!

We found out later that I was having a girl. I had known that I'd have a baby girl since I was in middle school and that her name would be Sheila, after my mother. I also looked forward to having a son like my mother. I thought we were on a tight budget before we had Sheila, but after her birth, it seemed that everything was a NO! I worked, and even though I said I'd help pay or we could save money each month, he would always say, "I'll think about it." Every time it became a no. He didn't believe you should be saving money to go or do anything if you still had bills to pay. I'm not talking about not paying your bills and taking the money to do other things. I mean, if you weren't rich and didn't have everything paid off, his thought is that you shouldn't go anywhere.

We didn't date, we didn't travel, we hardly went out to eat. Our focus was simply working and paying the bills. I became really bored and resented it!

When my grandparents became ill, I began working for myself. I did this for four years. During that time, funds were limited. However, working independently gave me the time and money needed to stay home with my daughter and take care of my parents. With my ex rotating, I spent the majority of my time at home, alone with my daughter. I later found out that he was volunteering to work over on many days he didn't have to. I was bored, frustrated, and lonely. When I begged for more time with him, to go out to reconnect as a couple, or to go to the couples retreats that happened all around us several times a year, we never went.

When I worked to pay for a weekend away in Concord, just forty-five minutes away from home, he barely spoke to me. No matter what, however, he thought I should always be excited to be with him sexually. It was hard for me because we didn't date each other anymore, and I not only had to work but I also lovingly cared for our child.

There was nothing to look forward to. I felt stuck and knew that our marriage wasn't in a good place. Anytime I brought this dilemma to him, he'd say sarcastically, "Do you want me to quit my job? I've got to work! No matter what, you're not happy." He was correct. I was not happy. I knew we could be a lot more as a couple and as a family. He was comfortable with his job, the house, and not being at home.

Our relationship suffered. I wanted to become more. I wanted more for our lives than just paying bills and working. I decided that I'd have a heart-to-heart with him. I really wanted to find a way to bring us back together.

I remember exactly what I was wearing, what he was wearing and which room in the house we were in. The silence was so thick in the air you couldn't cut it with a knife and I was there pleading with my ex again. I wanted to figure out why our communication had always been off and why we didn't do anything to mend our relationship.

We chose to zone out. He looked at me while I was standing there crying, shaking, and heartbroken because I could not find a way to connect with my husband. I tried so many times, and all he could hear from me was that I wanted to do something. He continued to let me know that my wanting to do these things would strain our finances, and he was tired. He did not feel like he had the time in his work schedule. I know it wasn't that pleasant for him to come home to a woman who was already tired from taking care of a home and a child. Remember, I was also working. I wanted to connect with my husband, but it seemed that the ways I wanted to connect to him did not appeal to him at all. I'm not sure, but I think the fact that we were married and I was obligated to have sex with him was the only connection required. I don't believe he ever considered WHY was I unhappy?

I'll never forget telling him, "what you won't do, someone else will." He still sat there in silence. This is where the conversation ended. At that moment, we began living separate lives under the same roof. No matter what I tried to do to close the gap between us, he just wasn't interested in me. At least, that's how I felt. I intentionally purchased new clothes and wore a new outfit every single day of the week. I also purchased new jewelry, did my makeup, and bought new perfume. He did not compliment once! Of course, I got compliments from others, but, the only man I wanted to really compliment me was my husband. It hurt, to say the least. It was as if I was a piece of lint in the corner somewhere. I went unnoticed for the entire week. I cried a lot when I was alone. I didn't understand what was wrong with me. Naturally, the compliments from others did give me a boost from time to time, but it still hurt.

Eventually, I gave in to my own happiness, or so I thought. I decided not to give too much thought about what anybody else would think or feel about my choices because I felt no one thought about me. I found myself playing into the advances of others. I had never believed that I would have ever stooped low enough to become a cheater. Until then, I had never cheated on anyone my entire life. I thought to myself, why at this time; at this age did I do this? I didn't realize what happened to me throughout those last years. I'm again talking to myself. You think I wouldn't say anything to my spouse about it, but I did immediately.

Looking back, I think that I thought my infidelity was going to be my way out. I thought my revelation would end my marriage. It didn't. There was no easy way out. My ex went back to his old job part-time while still working his full-time position. This is where his longtime friends worked and where I met him. Just the thought of him going back to that place and saying that he felt we might need the money was annoying. It was an easy second job but we didn't need as much money as he claimed because I worked! However, there were many things I didn't know that were going on with our finances.

I'm sure you're wondering why is she telling us all of this? What does this have to do with the scripture? I was so anxious to live out what I thought was a perfect dream, I had no clue of the price I was going to have to pay. Things were not perfect. They were not even good! We were definitely out of God's will. It felt like an out of body experience when things began to happen. We lied to each other and refused to tell each other things that we should not have withheld. We had no communication and our finances were jacked up! This was not the marriage that I had always dreamed of. In fact, this marriage was worse than my nightmare!

Let me reiterate that my ex became ill. His only income was his disability. Thus we were living on much less than we were accustomed to. However, we had earlier purchased two acres of land. I had paid for an acre and a half with my retirement money. I thought it was our way out of where we were living; our chance to start over. We had that land for about seven years.

Every single year I watched the land continue to go to waste. We didn't build on the land or in our relationship. That lot seems to symbolize everything that was wrong in my marriage. It was empty, lonely and purposeless. Then, I found out that I was pregnant. Of course, I knew the baby was not my ex's child. He and I had been living separate lives for quite some time at this point. We were two ships passing in the night that docked in the same place. That was all we were and I could not see us ever being more than that ever again.

Although this child I knew was not my ex's, I wanted to keep my baby. I knew that it would cost me my marriage, but wasn't it already over? My ex could not allow that to happen. He began a course of verbal abuse meant to break me down to my very core. He had already begun treating me with disrespect. He called me every name he could possibly think of as he tried to punish me for being "unfaithful" to a marriage that had long since been dead. My only reason for remaining in the sham of a marriage was to give my daughter her father. She was the consummate "daddy's girl", and I did not want to take that away from her. I didn't have a Dad or Mom outside of my grandparents, so I stayed, knowing that my marriage had been over for a very long time.

I found myself expecting another man's child and tied to a man who began to threaten me. He gave me an ultimatum. If I kept this baby, he would take my daughter away from me. He vowed to take me to court and fight for sole custody. I'd never been in trouble with the law and didn't think anything about the fact that he'd have to prove me to be an unfit mother. She was the only good thing that had come out of this marriage and he was going to take her away from me. I was the only person she had the time. I am not saying he was absent. What I mean is with him rotating and working so much he was always away and she was always with me.

My ex knew how much my daughter and I loved each other. I knew that the fact I was already carrying another man's child would come out in any divorce proceeding. I had no clue which way to go. I begged him to just go our separate ways. He wouldn't hear of it! He wanted to punish me as much as he could. Even though I assured him that I would never do anything to separate him from his daughter, he continued to threaten me with removing her from my life. All I wanted to do was walk away in peace if it was possible. It was not possible.

I always find out very early when I'm expecting. I found out that I was expecting at five weeks. I could not have an abortion until I was eight weeks pregnant. For three weeks, I begged and pleaded for my child's life. I could already feel the child growing inside me. I could hear its voice! I had no idea what beauty this child possessed; what beautiful song was being written within me. I didn't know what gifts God had already bestowed upon it. I imagined who and what this child would become. Then, I would look at my daughter's face, the one that I already held, whose face I knew better than my own and whose song I already sang. I couldn't lose her!

Just to make sure my life was living hell, my ex started calling my baby a bastard. He declared that "the piece of you know what" was only going to take a breath over his dead body. He told me that I either got an abortion and retained access to my daughter or keep the baby to lose my daughter forever! I was devastated! I never thought I'd find myself in a place where I had to decide which child I wanted to keep.

My ex continued with the verbal abuse and threats. Ironically, he was the person who drove me to have the procedure. If they still have my records from twenty years ago, they would state that the abortion was being done against my will. It was because the baby did not belong to my then-current husband. I did not want to have an abortion, but I was told that if I didn't, I would have my other child taken away from me.

Although they give you something that's supposed to relax you, something to help you forget what happens in that room, I remember every single moment. I still vividly remember crying on the table when they were prepping me. I remember feeling the procedure being done and hearing the sound of that machine, something like a vacuum cleaner, taking my baby out of me. It was like I was standing over myself watching all of this being done to me and my unborn child. Once the procedure was done, I wanted to know the sex of the baby. Of course, they wouldn't tell me. I couldn't get myself together. I had to stay much longer than most because they could not get my pressure to come down. I was just horrified by what had just happened. I was miserable and heartbroken. Then, to add insult to injury, the person who made me think that this was my only choice, was the one waiting on me. He drove me home and back to the nightmare I was living. Although there was no paperwork filed, our marriage had long ended.

I forget what they tell you. I think it's about 6 weeks afterward before you can be intimate with anyone. I believe, in my ex's mind, everything except our marriage was over. My baby was gone. He thought we could just pick up where we left off. He had no clue that I was never going to be the same again. He tried to be with me, and I just laid there. I was numb. I no longer had the feelings a wife should have for a husband.

I still cry for that child's life. My baby paid the price of my fear. Instead of choosing divorce and letting the pieces fall where they may. I think about how old it would be. I promised God at that moment that no matter what happened, no matter what my situation would be, if I found myself expecting again, I would not go through that process ever again. I had chosen my daughter. I also had chosen to bear the burden of this situation in my spirit until the day I stand before my Heavenly Father.

I told my ex-husband how I was feeling, how I was mourning my unborn child. I told him because he was so angry with me for not being affectionate towards him. I told him I would have rather he had just divorced me and thrown me out on the street then to have forced me to end my baby's life. He hadn't been the person who cheated and had gotten pregnant. He wasn't the person who made the decision to lay with somebody. I won't justify or make excuses for my actions. I will, however, say he shares in the weight of my decision to end a life.

From this point on we were only husband and wife on paper. I made him aware that I was only there for the sake of our daughter and that I had no loving feelings for him. I thought giving my daughter both of her parents under the same roof was going to be okay. Unfortunately, it made matters worse for me. I was still miserable. Looking back, I realized that I was tired. I was tired of where we lived, things were getting worse in the area. I was tired of being sad, I missed my child. I was tired of being lonely, he and I had no communication. Our relationship was over. I was tired of feeling confined, we had grown out of the space we lived in and it was moldy and in need of repair. I was tired of everything! I felt stuck. I felt as though I had nothing to look forward to.

One would think, after all of that, I would have found the strength to divorce my husband and move on with my life. I couldn't because, in my heart, I felt for him. He was my daughter's father, and he was sick, and I didn't want to leave him by himself. I did not pity him. I'd been a caregiver since the age of twelve and caring for those that meant a lot to me was normal for me. I'm glad that he was my spouse. I took that heart even deeper and felt that I needed to make sure that I was there, regardless of all that we had gone through, regardless of all that was said and done between us. Again I'm not going to sit here and share a lot of what I discovered during that time. That is his story to tell.

I thought I would be okay staying. I ignored myself as I took care of his needs. I lived to make sure he was okay. However, somewhere in this montage of caregiving I found myself expecting again. Because I had made a promise to God, it didn't matter that I was still in the marriage. I knew things would be more difficult as I still had to care for my ex and I needed to make sure I was still there for my daughter.

I went through hell carrying this baby. It was just my baby girl and me. It was painful to not be able to share this pregnancy with my husband or the child's birth father. I had to go through it pretty much alone, but my child's Nana is such a loving woman. Although she talked to me about the things that went wrong just like my mother used to, it was still her grandbaby. She wanted to give this child just as much love as she had all of her other grandchildren. I'm forever grateful to her for that. She has been the best grandmother a child could ever have. She even extended that same love to my daughter!

I concluded that it's time to finally do something with the land. We were never going to build on it, so this was a great time to sell. I knew that if we sold the land, we would find something else, and I didn't want to stay in my hometown anymore. I didn't go far, but I had already had enough of living where I was. When I suggested a move to my ex, of course, he didn't want to leave.

I spelled out my conditions to him. We had to sell the land and purchase a new place. This would have to be a fresh start with a clean slate for both of us. It could be that I had forgiven him for all of his transgressions and he continued to hold mine against me. We had made a deal to help each other. I thought we could, but things began to worsen.

As far as being a dad, he was the best any child could ever desire. Unfortunately, as a couple, we were not making it work. There had been too much water under the bridge. About four years later, I knew that we weren't going to make it. The environment grew more toxic with each passing year.

I didn't marry my husband to end up divorcing him. However, I refused to have my children grow up believing that what they were seeing between us was what marriage should be. It was hard, but I knew that divorce was best. I decided that it was time to get my life together. I knew that I wasn't happy in the marriage and I never would be. In addition, I began to understand that it wasn't up to my spouse to make me happy. I had to do that for myself.

He tried his best to hold on to the marriage but I knew things weren't going to get any better. They were more than likely going to get worse. I did not want us to end up hating each other.

Regardless of whether we were married or not, we shared a child. No matter what, I still loved him enough to be there for him. He had grown to love my last child as his own. I appreciated that. He and I are better friends and co-parents than we ever were as husband and wife.

As of today, he's never missed anything our children have ever done. The kids still see him several days out of the week. He has never been an "every other weekend" dad. He's always wanted to make sure that he had time with them. We've had all the challenges that most parents have, but we're making it work.

Since the divorce, have I made mistakes? Of course I have. My marriage taught me many things. That knowledge drives me to teach other couples how to make marriage work. I do my best to keep as many couples together as possible. If they are meant to be together, as long as the situation is not toxic, especially if they have children, I encourage them to find a way to date. I tell them to sit together and have the hard conversations before things get so bad that they refuse to listen to each other. Feed your heart, mind and soul every day.
I believe that if my ex and I had studied God's word together and continued to date each other many of our issues could have been avoided. Maybe I could have seen

things differently, had more faith and found a way to make my marriage work if I had been more spiritually centered. I believe I would have had a lot more patience and maybe just maybe I would have found a way to reach him.

As they say, hindsight is 20/20. I have learned a lot in the last twenty years. My journey has brought me tremendous understanding. I long to become the wife I was destined to be. I know so much more now and no matter how hard it may be, as long as God is first and as long as I purchase with a godly heart my prayers, I will do all I can to make sure I play my part. Although I have this longing, I'm learning not to be anxious and follow God's lead because his timing is perfect!

Thought of the Day

"Be anencourager, the world already has enough critics."
Unknown

When was the last time you encouraged someone?

Recall a moment someone encouraged you. How did it make you feel?

Love is...

1 Corinthians 13:4-8 NIV

4 Love is patient, love is kind. It does not envy, it does not boast, it is not proud. 5 It does not dishonor others, it is not self-seeking, it is not easily angered, it keeps no record of wrongs. 6 Love does not delight in evil but rejoices with the truth. 7 It always protects, always trusts, always hopes, always perseveres. 8 Love never fails. But where there are prophecies, they will cease; where there are tongues, they will be stilled; where there is knowledge, it will pass away.

The divorce was hard on all of us! Even me. I know I was the one who asked for the divorce, but it meant my two children would have to adjust to Mommy and Daddy living in separate places. Being the strong young lady she is, my daughter presented a strong front saying, Mom, we'll be okay. She was there to help me calm her brother. He cried for his dad every day until he adjusted to knowing that, although he lived in a different home, he would never leave him. He'd always be there for both of them.

My ex made it clear that he wanted to have time with the kids two nights a week. He never wanted to be an every other weekend dad. The attorney made it clear that if we could work out the schedule with the children on our own, they would not intervene. It was tough in the beginning. I had to get used to sharing my kids and having them away from me. That was extremely hard because I felt I couldn't protect them. But this is what every good dad goes through as well. Unfortunately, some moms don't get it right either. I had to trust that he would take good care of them, that he loved them in his own way just as much as I did. These verses are so critical to every life challenge. I had to put verse seven into practice after the divorce to provide a strong foundation for our children.

Whenever my co-parent and I have disagreements, I think about the fact that somehow we managed to stay together long enough to help each other through the most challenging times in our lives. He was awaiting his first kidney when I was about to give birth to my son. Everything about this situation was unimaginable. During my son's birth, my ex was there as I was there many times to help him get through quite a few medical challenges. I almost died during the delivery. My pressure bottomed out, and they almost had me on top of my head to get it regulated. When it was time to push for the last time or two, I was told to stop immediately.

I had no clue what happened. I asked uncontrollably what was wrong, later to find out they could see that the cord was wrapped around my baby's neck. They had to cut the cord before he was finally out. Guess who cut the cord? His "Dad". During this time of turmoil and all we had gone through, we were still there for each other in our worst times. I couldn't help but cry and feel the most awful guilt, shame, and remorse for all I was responsible for in the marriage.

I couldn't hold my son when he finally made it out. There was still much for them to do with me, so they gave him to my ex first. I couldn't begin to imagine the thoughts that were running through his head. He was there for the birth of another man's child. Maybe it was his way of saying he was sorry for all that happened with my last child. Regardless, he was there when no one else was. This is in no way me throwing shade at his birth father. I'm sure he had his own thoughts as well when he realized that I was going to keep my child. Again, not my story to tell.

From the moment my ex held "my" son, he became "our" son. He has been there for every event in his life, unless he was hospitalized. He's been Dad to BOTH of our children from day one and has never wavered!

We were married for sixteen years, together for nineteen years, but we didn't make it as a couple. Still, there was enough love between us to know when to let go. We had to let go so that there could still be love and respect between us. Sharing these truths are difficult but necessary. After all of these years, I still shed tears when I think about all of the hurt and pain we've been through. I understood the real meaning of this scripture when I had to learn to love myself again.

When we divorced, I had accepted that people on the outside would never understand all we went through. No matter what, I would be the person blamed for the end of my marriage. Everyone could SEE my sin. I had to learn that God had forgiven me even when no one else felt I was worthy of it.

But really, who is? I was not the first or the last person to fall from faith this fast, this hard, or this far! Still, I needed to work on myself from the inside out. No matter what I felt anyone else did to me or said about me, I had to remember, no one but God could put me in Heaven or Hell. I had to learn to love MYSELF again.

Since my divorce and as the past ten years have gone by, our children have been our primary focus. I've learned you can never over-communicate with each other as co-parents. There are times children will play one parent against the other if you aren't in constant communication with each other while they are minors. Our two didn't stand a chance at that. My baby is now 16, and he knows our truth.

Through the years, my ex and I have both dated other people. It was tricky in the beginning (while they were small). We learned to let whomever we dated to be a private matter unless it involved or affected our children. Speaking for myself, it was even more critical that I paid closer attention to that because the children lived with me. Did I get it right every time? No! But, the moment I knew things weren't right, that was the end of that relationship.

I've asked God to help me with the thought of anyone hurting my children because that wouldn't be pretty at all, to say the least. It's been ten years since our divorce. I haven't rushed the process. I do my best to love others and myself, as the scripture above states.

We can be our worst enemy. Negative self-talk is what the enemy wants. If he can get into our thoughts and cause us to think all we've done is who we really are, we're liable to live a life that will surely do us in. Don't let him.

Let God remind you with this verse that this is the love he has for you. This is the type of love that welcomes you back into His open arms. This is the love that He will use to heal your broken spirit. All He asks is that you do all you can to extend it to others. Loving others like this is a huge task at times, but He's given us all the strength we need to do it. Trust Him. Trust His love.

Thought of the Day

You carry so much love in your heart. Give some, to yourself."

R.Z

What was the worst time in your life?

Have you asked God and those you hurt for forgiveness, understanding that some may never forgive you?

What are some things you do for yourself to feed your mind and spirit positive energy?

My Joy...

Proverbs 22:6 NKJV

6 Train up a child in the way he should go, and when he is old, he will not depart from it.

My Sheila and Sidney! If I've done anything right at all, it's been giving them the best of me as a mother! I love them to no end! There is NOTHING that I wouldn't do to keep them safe and NOTHING I wouldn't do to keep them focused on living the life God has destined them to live. I didn't say they were perfect or that they wouldn't make mistakes. However, from the time they were old enough to understand me, I have told them I expect great things from them.

My Sheila

My baby girl and my princess! There's so much to share, so I'll try my best to hit the highlights. This one is feisty! She came into this world two weeks early and sounded her alarm as loud and proud as she could. Sheila Pauline Smith, lovingly named after both of her grandmothers, was born on April 12th. She was born on a Friday morning at 9:26 am. We tease her all the time about how she'd move a lot during Bible study and her dad and I would watch my shirt do the most hilarious dance.

We thought she was going to be a breach because she laid horizontally up until the last minute. Her favorite place to lay was on a nerve that would shoot pain down the left side of my body. I'd have to rub on my tummy and talk to her to wake her up until she moved into another position. Once she was head down, she was still face up. Lord, she was still doing her own thing. Sheila kept those little long skinny feet close to my ribs. It tickled a bit, but it was a weird feeling. Almost as weird as when she'd stretch and then draw her body up in a ball. But she was a healthy little princess, weighing in at 6 lbs. and 8 ½ ounces. Nothing calmed her but the sound of her Daddy's voice.

We read to her and played music for her in the womb, but his voice was the first familiar thing she heard. My heart melted. Little did I know that the way I carried her and all the little experiences we had, even sending me into false labor twice, would have a lot to do with her personality today. My grandparents, who reared me, were still living. Daddy (my granddad) was there first. Momma was at work but wasn't too far behind. My mother and sister- in- law were in the room with us. Yes, it was a family affair and has been since.

She was rotten! I can admit it now, LOL! Like I said, most of her time was spent with me. She hated taking naps because she knew she was missing something. No matter how tired she was, Sheila seemed to cry forever when I put her down. When she finally drifted off, she'd be out for four hours every time. During her naps, I got a lot done, but I also had to learn to rest with her. She has always had a strong will. This paid off for her as she got older.

When Sheila entered elementary school, she constantly got into trouble for talking. I thought she did not know the rules. She proudly said that she knew them and then recited them. I'd say so you decided to still do it your own way, huh? Again, Sheila proudly and respectfully answered, "Yes ma'am!". Goodness gracious, this one! This, too, served her well later in life!

Something about being a caregiver to her dad at such an early age and knowing just as much as I did at five years old, made her very mature. She got her first cell phone at 9 years old (Disney phones for children). As a caregiver she understood very early, the importance of following instructions.

Although she had a strong will, she was always a very respectful child. Sheila's real character and personality began to settle as early as 3rd and 4th grades. She remained on either A/B honor roll or straight A Honor Roll from day one. Due to our family's financial struggles, Sheila couldn't attend the many scholarly summer camps that required tuition payments. However, she worked extremely hard to maintain her GPA and deserved to attend. At the age of 15, one of her educators contacted Mary Baldwin College (a private all-girls college in Staunton, VA) on Sheila's behalf.

We had never heard of the college. They began to send us information about their PEG program, Program of the Exceptionally Gifted. This program allowed young girls between the age of 12-16 to enter college, not continue high school, based on their academics.

We visited the college to learn more about the program and the cost, of course. I really didn't have the heart to tell her "no" before I gave God a chance to show me how it could happen. This college was four hours away from home. No one else, family or church friends (I worked for a church at this time) could see how in the world I would even consider this. She was only 15! This was a time that I had to stand completely alone in the matter. They shared that the girls had their own PEG dorm, their own security and transportation, and topped it with a strict curfew. It definitely eased my mind a little, but still...four hours away! Some of the cost was cushioned by grants and scholarships. Still, I had to cover a few thousand for books and other fees. I had no clue how it was going to happen.

I shared the news with my family, tried to explain what I had learned, but I was promptly told, "I can't afford to help with that." It was college. It came about three years earlier than planned, but she had well-earned this beautiful opportunity. We found that all Sheila lacked was one math course, the SAT and ACT, and she could skip 11th and 12th grade and enter college once she was accepted. That gave me at least a year to prepare. I knew we could pull it off if it was God's will.

I then had a long talk with Sheila. I wanted to see how she really felt about it all. Was she excited? What about being so far from home? Was she really ready for college work? Well, I learned as the regular pace of school always seemed too easy for her, a bit boring. Was this really happening? Yes, it was happening! Sheila's response? "Mom, I'm ready!"

I had to be real with her that outside of a friend or two of mine, no one else supported her going. We talked about all that she's learned and will learn about life's challenges, to think twice or even three times before making any decision. And yes, we had the mom lectures about not "embarrassing your family! Remember you are a Smith/Farmer, and we're all strong people. Represent us well if not better than we've ever been!".

Sheila worked hard her sophomore year of high school, passed her math course, performed as well if not better than most seniors on the SAT and ACT, and received her letter of acceptance. I balled! I cried so hard because I knew my time at home with my baby girl had been cut short. I was proud of her; how in the world could I say no, although everyone else was against it?

We, family and friends, gathered to pray for her and send her off with what we could. She did more than make our family proud; Sheila soared! She had more than a few challenges along the way and still soared. She was on the Dean's List every year! She began to come out of her shell. She worked in a few positions most upperclassmen would hold. She found her love of film there. She traveled quite a bit too. Her most memorable trip was to Prague! This was all due to God's help, financially and spiritually, every step of the way! No matter what was needed, He made a way. At times, He even used people who didn't even know us. I often talked to Sheila about her faith and doing all she could to stay close to God, remembering His promises and thanking Him for making ways.

Sheila graduated at 20 years old! She took a year break and then attended UNC Wilmington, where at twenty-four, she completed her second degree. I don't know how many times I've told her how proud I am of her. She has worked on several films and met many superstars. God has truly blessed her! I'm proud to be her mother!

My Sidney

My baby boy; my prince! Carrying this young man took a lot of strength and courage, physically and spiritually. I'm blessed to be his mother! I faced a heck of a lot while carrying him. There were tons of judgments because of how he came to be, but he was flesh of my flesh and bone of my bone. I had to fight for us both. Remember, as mothers, we have no clue who we are carrying in our wombs. He was born on April 2nd; Friday morning at 7:33am. I will share a piece I wrote in Sherilyn Michelle Bennett's "Boy Book" this past Spring concerning our country's racial tension is continuing to experience with the horror many of our black and brown boys are faced with. We had to write a letter to America as well as to our fellow mothers of black and brown boys:

America, did you know?

My handsome young black King! When I look at Sidney at the age of 16, standing 6'2", in a size 14 shoe and a grown man's body, I still see that 9 pound, 2 ½ ounce baby boy. He was such a beautiful and happy baby! His hair was so long and curly. Everyone thought he was a girl no matter how many sports outfits and ball caps we dressed him in. There were only two looks Sidney gave. It's still that way today, serious with eyes fiercely squinted to look straight through someone to figure out who you really are or a huge smile with laughter. Overall he was and still is a happy child/young man! Sidney began talking at nine months and walked after his first birthday. By the time he was two years old, he and I started sharing our first set of conversations about God, how He created him with wonderful gifts and purpose. He knew even then that God had something special in store for his life.

Sidney's entire mission was to find out his purpose and do his best to fulfill it. His Nana, Carolyn Wright, discovered his music gift when he was 1 year and 8 months old. He started drumming on a full set of drums at the age of two and discovered many other instruments. Sidney has a vast appreciation for music. It's how he breathes. Through music, he shares who he is with the world. He's a gentle giant. He strives to let nothing get in his way of becoming who he feels God intended him to be, to have, or become.

Those who don't know Sidney, who judge him and want to harm him because of his skin color. It doesn't seem to put fear in his heart. His focus is on living the life he was destined to live. I've always told my son from the start, "I expect great things from you. You are loved, and you are given something extra special that only you can bring into this world." He knows that. He believes it too, and rightfully so!

Since Sidney's birth, I've been fervently praying for him. This world still can't appreciate the beauty of all the differences we as a human race share—the color of our skin, our culture, how our black history shapes our present and future. I've always told Sidney God built him as he is for a reason; his broad shoulders and muscular back, his height, his full lips, his broad nose, his piercing eyes, his tightly coiled, curly hair, those size 14 feet, and solid body which is like a brick wall when you run into him. Like many other young black Kings, he carries the weight of a world that still doesn't see him as a strong human being, mentally and physically. They see him first as a threat, without even getting to know who he really is.

As he continues to grow up to become the man God would have him to be, I know the enemy's job is to keep him off course from his purpose. Who's the enemy? The spirit of others who hate him merely because of his beautiful bronzed, sun kissed skin. Or, because he's taller than most and built with such strength, he doesn't even know he has. Sidney's still learning more about this world filled with people who don't know him yet want to take the very breath he breathes. The enemy is also that voice that whispers negativity and doubt in his ear, telling him that his life doesn't matter, he can't achieve success because he's black. Statistics say otherwise. America, you have no clue who this young King is! With all that Sidney has accomplished at such a young age, drummer, baritone saxophonist, guitarist, music producer, hard-working employee, and teen entrepreneur. There is so much more he has to accomplish, so much he hasn't tapped into.

Because of America's hate, there is so much I've had to teach him. Hopefully, this teaching will protect him and safely get him back home, where he is loved and cared for. If it's anything to do with police officers stopping him for ANY reason, I've asked Sidney to please not plead his case at the time, to comply. Since the death of so many of our black Kings, I can't say that would even save his life. I've asked Sidney to try to relax and to be sure to call his attorney first!

I keep an attorney retained just for my son's protection. America, please give his life and many other young black Kings a chance to show you who they REALLY are! Anything and anyone that intends to rob our young black Kings of God's promises THAT is the enemy! The good book says in Jeremiah 29:11, "For I know the plans I have for you," declares the Lord, "plans to prosper you and not to harm you, plans to give you hope and a future." Their lives have a purpose.

I'm praying fervently that I get to see at least a glimpse of what God has for my son. I see him with a beautiful family living a full life of love, joy, and legacy. I see children and a wife. My hope is that Sidney looks back over my life as far as he can, all that I'm striving for, and all

I've shared with him to master the lessons I've tried to teach him. Although I'm the mom, I've learned a lot from him already. Still, that loving and happy go lucky attitude is at the core of who he is. Things that others do or say, as long as they don't harm him physically, he could care less. Sidney doesn't let what others say or do get him out of your character. I pray he keeps it that way! I pray he can do what makes him happy and feel good about it as long as it's godly and it doesn't harm others. He believes in prayer. There are times now that Sidney reminds me to pray about my challenges. Sidney has grabbed my hand while driving or at home, it doesn't matter, to pray on the spot. God has brought us through a lot! I pray as he gets older to please don't forget to do that in his time of need or when he feels challenged. He tends to live in the moment and has always been the life of the party from an early age. Oh, how I pray he continues to do that. God has only promised us the very breath we're taking at the moment. We must make every moment count, not spend it in hatred.

To my fellow mothers of these young, black, and gifted sons we have, please remember they are their own person. The presence of their father or a positive male role model, if he's willing, is critical to our son's identity. He has a strong desire to know from whence he came and needs guidance into manhood. I've learned that no matter how great a mother I try to be; I can't fill that void. My son's dad is very active in his life. He has been since his birth and even after our divorce. Co-parenting isn't always easy, but it's essential to my son's physical, emotional, and spiritual growth. It gives our young kings a strong foundation of support. If they can see how their black fathers or black male role models have navigated this world, we live in a world where they still aren't valued or protected.

I'm learning as he gets older to listen more, allow him to share his feelings about life no matter what it's about. They are walking around outside of the home, going to school and/or work in a world that cares nothing about how he feels or what he thinks. Our sons need a safe and sacred place to land. Hopefully, this is one way to keep them from holding all the hurt and pain they hold inside from feeling less than a human being.

To my fellow moms who have fatherless young black Kings, maybe they are deceased, walked away, or the father simply doesn't want to be a part of his son's life. For whatever the reason, I feel we must watch who we choose to have in our lives as a male role model. The men you have in your life as a friend, significant other, male relatives, etch. They influence our sons negatively or positively. There's no in-between. The older my son gets; the more time he likes to spend around the family's men. Does it mean he loves his motherless, no? He simply is trying to identify with other men, to learn more about manhood. My belief is that as a woman, I know nothing about manhood. I can only share with him and tell him how I feel a woman should be treated. He gets his practice with that from myself, his sisters, his Nana and Granny, his aunties, and female cousins. But, none of us as women can show him anything about being a man. It's critical to have the right male role models in his life. My desire is for Sidney to become who God would have him be, not like anyone else. Yet, his genetics, some of his mannerisms, and how he navigates life sometimes mimics some of the characteristics of the men he's closest to. So be careful, fellow moms.

That being said if your relationship with his father is toxic. Maybe, his father has also endured a cold hard America, and he still is carrying it. Don't treat your young black King, your son, negatively due to his father's mistakes or decisions. His life could be totally different.

Continue to inspire your son, lift him up by reminding him that he's special, that he's chosen to bring something into this world that only he can.

If there is past trauma, some life-altering event that has taken place in your son's life, and you can see that he is no longer the ray of "sonshine" you've always known him to be. Please, encourage counseling. Take your son to counsel. So many of our kings hold their hurt and pain deep inside. We have taught them to "not be soft." "Take it like a man." That's partly why the suicide rates of young black men are rising. According to the Journal of Community Health, black boys ages 13-19 from 2001-2017, the rate rose 60 percent. Mental health is crucial for us all, especially with everything America is currently going through. There seem to be no changes. Hearing of a black man's untimely and unauthorized death several times a day has caused severe trauma in our young black kings' lives who have just begun. The outlook is so grim. It's heartbreaking and unfair. Moms, we must pray! We must pray and stand together to hopefully help find ways to protect, encourage, equip, and empower our young black Kings. We can't give up, and we can't give in. We must believe the TRUE KING, OUR KINGS OF KINGS, will bring about a change in our country, in this world. Be steadfast, knowing that we were truly bought for a price. God will not leave us. He's still here and will deliver us!

I love you, my young black Kings! I love you, my fellow mothers, my Queens! Many blessings! Hopefully, my book will still have relevance in your life somehow or for years to come. Hopefully, both of my children have continued to do well. Yes, they're going to make some mistakes and experience some challenges along the way.

My prayer is that if I'm gone, and you see them out in this old world we live in, encourage them as you would your own. Pray for them and give them encouraging words to continue this journey. Don't give up on them! This is what I hope we do for all our children. The thought of not being with them one day is too hard to dwell on. I hope that I have taught them well and have lived a life, for example, before I pass on. I pray there is such a legacy left behind that my love will reach many generations beyond them and out in the rest of the world.

Thought of the Day

"In my life, you are the sun that never fades and the moon that never wanes. Shine on my child."

Anonymous

Parent or not, in what way can you positively influence a child's life?

Moving Forward...

Habakkuk 2:2-3

2 Then the Lord answered me and said:

"Write the vision and make it plain on tablets,

that he may run who reads it.

3 For the vision is yet for an appointed time,

but at the end, it will speak, and it will not lie.

Though it tarries, wait for it; because it will

surely come, it will not tarry.

Ecclesiastes 3:1-8

There is a time for everything,

and a season for every activity under the heavens:

2

a time to be born and a time to die,

a time to plant and a time to uproot,

3

a time to kill and a time to heal,

a time to tear down and a time to build,

4

a time to weep and a time to laugh,

a time to mourn and a time to dance,

5

a time to scatter stones and a time to gather them,

a time to embrace and a time to refrain from embracing,

6

a time to search and a time to give up,

a time to keep and a time to throw away,

7

a time to tear and a time to mend,

a time to be silent and a time to speak,

8

a time to love and a time to hate,

a time for war and a time for peace.

There is no better way to end this part of our journey together with this book than this. When you read it, slow down. Let every single word of His Word sink in. There is no way of getting around it. Look at your life as I have mine. I just left my only brother and a cousin of ours on the Farmer's side. As we stood there saying our goodbyes, another cousin on the Gill's side stopped, and we spoke and shared words of love as she drove off. Have you ever looked at my face when I share pictures of my family on social media? No matter what side of the family they are on, I have the biggest smile on my face because WE ARE FAMILY!!! Yes, it's intense when we share the same blood. Still, there are people in my life that were either married into our families, shared children in our families, or were such lifetime family friends that we blend so well you couldn't tell who was blood-related or what I call "love" related!

In this book, I have shared a lot that, for some, it seems I'm trying to call people out. That's not true. Some may feel I should have kept it all to myself and carried it to my grave. Well, how's that working for a lot of our families? Many of us still don't know all of our relatives, much less who we really are or where we originated. Yes, it saves face for the moment. What I mean is, all the parties involved may not be embarrassed or found out or the moment. But, it always seems to be the innocent people involved that get hurt the most. I've been on both sides of that spectrum. Honestly, I'd rather be the one hurt than the one hurting others. As the scripture says, "there's a time to weep and a time to laugh." I try to find a reason to laugh and make others laugh rather than to cry. It's also a reminder that we're going to grieve some things in life; a torn relationship, a loss of opportunity, a child, a friendship, etc. This scripture is so profound because although I've wanted to have the right side of each part of this scripture to be true for me, oh have I felt and experienced each one of the challenging or sad parts of this scripture. With Covid-19 still running rampantly through our country, whenever I get to see anyone of my relatives now, I'm even more excited than when I last saw them. So many of our family and friends have passed on. I realize that I haven't spent enough time with all of my family and friends, no matter what side of the family you're on. I love you! Truly I do! I know we've had our disagreements and so many challenging moments. Some of us feel forgotten, mistreated, left so alone, and at times an outcast. But I beg of you today, if I have made any of you ever feel that way, it was definitely not my heart.

Here comes transparency...there are times I was dealing with financial burdens that I didn't share. It kept me focused on nothing but paying what bills I could and feeding and clothing my children. Again, I'm not slighting their fathers. My co-parent has given his all for our two. They have their own households and challenges. I can only speak from personal experience. Whether you're a single father or mother, even with a co-parent, sometimes, no matter what help you're receiving outside of what you earn (I've always worked), it still isn't enough. I didn't ask for help at times because I knew a lot of you were dealing with your own financial burdens. But, I have never been ashamed of standing in line for food giveaways to feed my children when what I had wasn't enough. I've been on SNAP when I was laid off and when the positive I found still didn't bring enough in to cover it all. I've never abused the system, but I tell you, when you don't have it and your children depend on you, you've got to do something to provide. At least you SHOULD! There were times you didn't see me because, with all the stress and changes that were going on, I didn't feel my best, nor look my best. I feared being talked about or shamed. I also felt a tremendous amount of shame with all that had taken place in my life, although I know we all have something in our lives we're not proud of about our journey. Please, once this pandemic is over, keep in mind that we all will look different. Some of us are better, and some are working to get back to ourselves, physically and mentally. So, don't judge. Just welcome everyone with open arms when the time comes.

Whatever has happened in the past, ask God to help and give you the strength to let it go! Writing this book has taken me a year and a few months. I found there was so much I still harbored in my heart. I've cried so many tears. I've had to consult with my mentor/editor many times. Many times she's put my writing to a halt, and we prayed on the spot. I've shared a lot of this process with my best friend, Angie, and my lifetime friend Elliott. Without their prayers and constant godly love, I wouldn't have made it through. They have been there in all my most challenging moments of life. This scripture, Lord is everything! It plainly states we're going to go through some things. There will be life events we planned and some we didn't. No matter what, remember, whatever God's will is, THAT is what will be. The moment I understood that and accepted that my life with God's help has become more manageable.

Again, there is a time.... yes, Lord! I ask all of you publicly, family and/or friends if I have done anything to harm you or hurt you in any way. Please forgive me! It doesn't matter that we haven't spoken in years or seen each other in years. It still bothers me. I want to leave in my time with a clear heart and mind knowing that I have made things right. I want my children to know this must be done, not always to excuse the other party of their wrongdoing, but to allow you to live a life free from grudges and the strength and will to move on. Should we all be up close and personal in each other's lives again as before?
In some cases, no. It might be best to love from afar. It's not to slight someone, but again, it may be the end of a season. Is the love still there, sure. But whatever God has

for you to do in this life must be done, and any one or thing that keeps you from that must be removed. Everybody is not ordained to be with you on the next level God takes you.

Life comes at us hard and fast. We are ready, and there are times we had no clue it was coming, but God! I have learned that God is and will continue to be right there with us in EVERY season of our lives, whether it be a season you're being blessed in or a season you're experiencing sorrow in. He's always there! God has never failed me and never left me alone. I've lost so many people in my life, especially by death, others live far away, some are dealing with life's challenges as I have, but God! He's a Keeper! He's kept me when I had no clue I needed to be kept. God created every season! He knows precisely what is to come, and He's equipped you to deal with it all in His strength. I ask all of us to dive into His word more.

There's not a promise yet that is there that He hasn't kept for me. I don't know what season of life you're in right now, but don't live it without Him! No matter what season it is, don't stop dreaming. Make sure you write the vision for your life, put it on paper (vision board). Ask God what His will is for you and your vision. Ask Him to show it to you. I promise if it's Him you hear from; it will be apparent. Realize that the season to love hard is upon us! Yes, I promise you you'll get hurt a time or two, but leave it up to God to set the record straight. He always does in HIS timing, not ours. The time is NOW to leave a legacy! I'm not talking about just financially. I mean spiritually as well for generations to come. How do you want to be remembered? Especially if you have children. How do you want them to remember you? What can you do now to touch your family and others that will touch many generations to come? It can be a scary thought when you are already past your 40s, I know! Life, Love,

Legacy...how we live it, how we do it, and how we build it matters more than anything!
Be blessed y'all! I love you!

As I look over my life, with all the things that ever happened, The Good, the bad ugly...I think that I was looking for a love that I had never experienced. Yes, my grandparents did a heck of a job raising two children that were utterly traumatized and left as orphans, not purposely, though. Our family was there for us as much as possible, but I just cannot explain the hole left in a child's heart without having their parents. Their mother who birthed them who gave her life to bring them here, and the father who was supposed to protect them failed. They were children still and hadn't even mastered living for themselves, and they had us. I have no idea what it feels like to be loved and cherished by a man that wants nothing from you. He just wants to love you, protect you, and show you what you mean to him. To teach you all that he can to keep you from falling prey to other men. My ex did the best that he could. I believe that I did as well with what I had in me. And yes divorced and have dated a few different types of men, although I've had people that cared for me still even though I've never experienced it, I can tell by looking at other young ladies who did have their fathers there for them that that kind of love is like none other. The only person that comes close to that for me, it seems, is God. I must admit, being human, though and not having him physically here to touch me to hold me to encourage me to spend that kind of time with me is hard. But again, he's always there, and my soul can rest in that! He's fought my battles, He's provided for me, and He still loves me even when I'm at my worst. He's never left me, and I'm forever grateful! My prayer is That I live the life He intended for me. Letting everything else go that's behind me, I will move forward.

NOTES

NOTES

NOTES

Made in the USA
Middletown, DE
17 October 2024